PERFORM LIKE A ROCK STAR

AND STILL HAVE TIME FOR LUNCH

PERFORM LIKE A ROCK STAR

AND STILL HAVE TIME FOR LUNCH

ORNA W. DRAWAS

FOREWORD BY MATTHEW SZULIK

To Randy,
who taught me that to be a rock star
is the only way to be.

ACKNOWLEDGEMENTS

I'd like to thank the many rock stars who helped me make this book possible.

Jeremy Drawas - You were the first to believe in me and with that you helped me to believe in myself. Thanks for your willingness to help me get started on the path, your constant encouragement, positive feedback and support every step of the way. As my son, you fill me with immense joy and pride.

Carly Drawas - It was you who said, "Mom, if you don't get out of your comfort zone you'll never grow" and made me wonder — 'Now, who's the grown-up here?' Thanks for encouraging me to live my dream and reminding me that falling down doesn't matter; it's the getting up that counts.

Dafna Lebow, MD - You are my hero! You have shown me that a true rock star has big ideas, high hopes and the passion to make even the wildest dreams a reality. This book was your idea. Who else but you would have thought that I could do it?

Irit Karsh, MD — You've been my lifelong idol and are the epitome of life/work balance. It takes a rock star to be a doctor, a mother, a tennis player, a golfer, and a great skier. Thanks for showing me how to do a great job and still have time for a *gourmet* lunch.

Patricia Ross, PhD - Such a talented and dedicated editor who helped me develop a real personality throughout these chapters. Your additions (and deletions) added clarity and spirit to the book.

Alan Hebel and Ian Shimkoviak – The creative duo at the Book Designers who understood rock star status and created the perfect book cover and layout design for future rock star readers.

Nichol Ashworth - Your cartoons rock! Thanks for your never-ending creative ideas....too many to use in this one book, so I have saved some for next time.

Gregg Martucci and Hal Horowitz—You are true music aficionados, who brought music to my ears and to the chapters of this book.

Matthew Szulik – The kid from the sleepy fishing town of New Bedford who built a company based on free software and became the Ernst & Young Entrepreneur of the Year... you are what these pages are about. Thank you for graciously contributing the Foreword of this book.

Randy Drawas - My husband and partner in life - to you I offer my heartfelt appreciation for helping me maintain the high standards you set for yourself in everything you do. Your insight, stories, editing, design ideas, collaboration and support have impacted me personally, and are evident in every page of this book.

CONTENTS

- **Not Everything's a Priority**
Figure out the relevant over the irrelevant.

- **Oh No! It's Five Already?**
How'd the day pass you by?

CHAPTER 6
BRING ORDER TO CHAOS

- **Make a List . . . Check It Twice!**
Turn to-do's into actions.

- **Give Your Boss a Dose of Reality**
Does your boss know what you're working on?
If not — big mistake!

- **Two Tickets to Paradise**
Paradise awaits the masters of the 80/20 Rule.

- **Know Your Priorities**
What could you get done in two hours?

CHAPTER 7
IT'S NOW OR NEVER

- **Master Procrastinator**
Who do you think you're fooling?

- **Three Easy Steps to Defeat Procrastination**
Simply apply it and it works . . . or your money back!

CHAPTER 8
ONE OF THESE DAYS IS NONE OF THESE DAYS

- **Learn to Love Deadlines**
Deadlines are not your enemy.

CHAPTER 9
COPING IN A SANDSTORM OF INTERRUPTIONS

- **Please Just Stop Talking!**
Manage disruptions without sacrificing relationships.

- **Just Say No**
Be nice, but know your priorities.

CHAPTER 10
USING THE POWER OF OTHERS

- **The Art of Delegating**
Captain Kirk ran a tight ship.

- **Delegate the Results, Not the Process**
. . . Then get out of the way.

CHAPTER 11
ARE YOU STONED OR JUST CHECKING E-MAIL?

- **Air, Water and E-mail**
Can't live without it, but who's in control?

- **Are You Stoned or Just Checking E-mail?**
Checking e-mail is more disruptive than smoking marijuana.

- **The 14 Holy Commandments of E-mail**
Find your way to e-mail heaven.

- **How Much is that E-mail in the Window?**
What is e-mail costing you?

CHAPTER 12
TO MEET OR NOT TO MEET, THAT IS THE QUESTION

- **Meetings Get a Bad Rap for Good Reason**
Why good meetings go wrong.

- **The Seven Rules for Productive Meetings**
Make meetings matter.

CHAPTER 13
THE PRESENT

- The Gift of Time
Make the most of it.

PART III – A CULTURE OF PEAK PERFORMANCE

CHAPTER 14
RAISING EVERYONE'S GAME

- The Road to Peak Performance
How do you get there from here?

- Create a New Kind of Culture
Make it fun. Make it rewarding.

CHAPTER 15: A PROGRAM FOR PERFORMANCE

- Personal Development or Team Training
Make Peak Performance Real.

- The Peak Performance Program

FOREWORD

by *Matthew Szulik*

CHAIRMAN, RED HAT

2008 ERNST & YOUNG ENTREPRENEUR OF THE YEAR

There is no secret recipe. No cookie cutter formula for life-long success. I have met hundreds of highly success people in my lifetime from presidents of countries to some of the planet's wealthiest individuals. Few if any were born into their success. Most have seen life as a journey. Their common denominator to success has been their individual passion for their chosen craft. All had failed not simply once, but many times. And surprising as it may be to some, few would offer that achieving financial success was a goal. Almost all would say that becoming the best one could be at what they did was the driving factor in their success.

I am one of those people. Born in a humble place, the fishing town of New Bedford, Massachusetts. A pretty good student. Not a great one. Most of the time, I was the student that teachers had to correct and discipline. No MBA. I was always curious.

From 1998 to 2008, as the CEO of Red Hat, I led the transformation of a magazine publisher into becoming a global enterprise software company that came to be listed on the New York Stock Exchange with over a billion dollars of cash in the bank. Red Hat today has almost a billion in sales and a market capitalization of four billion dollars. More interesting, Red Hat has built its business selling free software. That's right, selling free software and competing successfully against Microsoft. In 1997 when I told my Dad I was joining a young start up called Red Hat, he suggested that I get a good job like my older brother at IBM. Instead, I chose to reach for the stars.

Failure. More than my fair share. Wow, try walking into some of the most elite venture capital companies in the world telling them you want to raise $10 million to fund a company that sold free software and compete against an industry monopoly like Microsoft. After the laughter and rejection, I would pick up my bag and move on to the next investor. Failure was not an option. Sure enough, I found the investors and they've been handsomely rewarded for the risk they took.

I meet many people who look back on their lives and regret their professional decisions. Some wish they had become pastry chefs instead of lawyers. Or wish they became teachers instead of bankers. Some people retreat to a life of conformity and wake up wondering how they wasted those important years of their lives doing uninspiring work.

I say, don't wait. The trap to climb out of the daily grind gets deeper as you age. Start now. You are talented. You have the passion. Heck, if a guy from New Bedford can make it selling free software, what's holding you back?

It's time to start living your life and performing like a rock star.

—*Matthew Szulik*

ON THE COVER OF ROLLING STONE
DR. HOOK AND THE MEDICINE SHOW, 1973

Wanna see my picture on the cover
Wanna buy five copies for my mother
Wanna see my smilin' face
On the cover of The Rolling Stone.

INTRODUCTION

If you want to go places in the increasingly crazy, fast paced, competitive, ever-changing business world... all the while opening yourself up to true enjoyment and elation in your life... then you've got to think, act and perform like a rock star. And if you can get to that place, and still have time to enjoy all that surrounds you, I'd say, 'well; now we've got something to talk about.'

Don't get me wrong. The fame and fortune that comes from being a rock star is all good in my book. But, in the bigger, broader scheme of things, it can also be something else. It can be about becoming a true leader, a real mover, and quite simply, someone who people can count on to makes things happen. Someone who can deliver results, and just plain 'get 'er done.' When you perform like a rock star, something special happens. People notice you. People come to admire you. And people want to be associated with you.

When you make this happen in your life, things naturally open up. The possibilities become greater. The places you can go are boundless. And you begin to feel like you are making a difference in your life and the life of others. How good would it be to feel like you were a rock star?

That's what this book is all about. Inside these pages you can uncover ways to attain whole new levels in your own personal *peak performance* that can bring greater success and a much deeper sense of fulfillment, personal joy and satisfaction in your work life... still have time for lunch and so much more.

1

THE OPENING ACT

Humor me — let's imagine that moment at work when you've had a real personal breakthrough.

For starters, you're being incredibly efficient and effective.
You are achieving true results and being recognized.
You have a newfound sense of control over your life.
You're feeling energized and are less stressed.
You have a deeper sense of personal pride and confidence.
You're on top of your game; the master of your own destiny.
Wow!

This is what it's like to be a Peak Performer! A Rock Star.

How would your life be if you were all that? Would it be exciting and empowering? Would you feel passionate about what you were doing and where your career is heading? Would you crave finding deep satisfaction every day in everything you do?

OK, now stop for a nanosecond. Let's switch gears.

Think about your own reality. How often do you have the opportunity to play out the scene above; bring out the peak performer side of who you are? My guess is — not often enough, and possibly not at all. Unfortunately, most people I know are like my dear friend Jodi.

Jodi's success didn't come easily. She worked long hours, focused on details to get her job done and never accepted mediocrity from herself or those around her. Within six months of joining a premier financial management firm, she was promoted to Vice President of Strategic Planning. She helped the firm win the biggest account in its 30-year history and was the center of major buzz in the industry. My childhood friend was feeling on top of the world.

As Jodi's career progressed, the company won several impressive industry awards and was attracting to its staff a whole new level of clients as well as the brightest minds in the industry. Jodi loved her job and was great at it. Her co-workers and her boss appreciated her efforts and Jodi felt confident, happy and in control of her life. Her daily activities provided an outlet to showcase her talents and her busy schedule made her feel fulfilled, proud and accomplished.

Suddenly, and not knowing exactly how it happened, Jodi noticed that her life, and those euphoric feelings of success, had somehow slipped away. Her To-Do List got longer and longer, her stress level got higher and higher, all the while the quality of her work seemed to suffer. Everything became a priority. Most things didn't seem to get done, or, for that matter, done well. Too much to do in too little time. Days were filled with the distractions of e-mail, meetings, interruptions and paperwork, leaving Jodi feeling like she was spinning her wheels and getting nowhere fast.

Somehow, she lost control and that's when we met for dinner. Jodi was wondering "Does it have to be this way? Can't I be a rock star and still have time for lunch?"

YOUR OWN PERSONAL REVOLUTION

Let's talk about you for a minute. Hopefully you're really busy at work with a ton of stuff to do every minute of every day. If you consider yourself a serious professional, you're probably working very hard. You may even be working inordinately long hours plus sporadically on weekends. My question to you, and please come clean, is: are you working on the right things? Are you working on the things that are going to propel you and your career (and your life, for that matter) forward? Or are you busy focusing on the many hundreds of random activities that are actually inconsequential to your work? Are you getting the results that matter or are you simply very efficient at getting things done? Honestly, there can only be one right answer.

I believe it is absolutely possible for a person to have way too many things to do and still function with higher than normal productivity, all with a clear head and a positive sense of control. The key is knowing what the right things are—those activities that can bring real meaningful results and move you closer to achieving your goals—accelerating you on your path to peak performance.

It's not easy. We get bogged down in details and distractions. Our boss imposes unrealistic deadlines. Our co-worker stops by to ask a favor or to socialize (after all, work can be a pleasant social environment). Then there are the constant demands of e-mail and the magnetic draw of Facebook, MySpace, Twitter, blogs, online games, and texting, not to mention meetings and conference calls and, well, you can add more I'm sure. It's a small wonder that anything gets done! Let's face it; there are many forces that stand in your way of achieving true greatness.

Then there's the constantly shifting ground we stand on. I often ask successful business professionals if they are doing exactly what they were originally hired to do. I have yet to meet someone who answers yes. The companies we each work for, and the world that surrounds us is constantly shifting, always evolving and being transformed. In this world of ours priorities are continually changing as well. What you were hired to do may not be considered important anymore. So it is clear that if you are smart, you will continually adjust and keep your eye on the ball. As the ball moves, so must you. Be flexible enough to recognize it and be prepared to move where you can make the greatest impact.

Needless to say, your ability to break through the noise and clutter is one of the keys to achieving your peak performance. And, if you're like most of my clients, you often feel like you're swimming upstream. I find the natural human tendency is to "Major in Minors" – meaning doing a great job working diligently on things that, in many cases, don't really add up to much. To have what can be classified as a truly productive day and find true happiness in your work, you must be willing to swim against this tide and keep focused on those things that can make an absolute difference in your work and ultimately your life.

So, with that, let me first thank you for picking up this book. In exchange for your curiosity, I will share with you many of the truths I have come to know about how to be your personal best in moving you and your career forward. I will demonstrate that by choosing the relevant over the irrelevant, and by selecting those tasks that deliver long-term benefits from those that are fun, easy, and provide immediate gratification, you can fast track your career and your life, and begin moving ahead with greater momentum than you ever thought possible.

When others see your accomplishments, they will take notice and gravitate towards the success you create all around you. You now stand poised to create a *personal results revolution*. It begins today and it's all about creating a personal culture of Peak Performance.

WARNING!

PERFORM LIKE A ROCK STAR will not tell you what your personal breakthrough goals should be to propel your career forward. Rather, this book provides you with a solid approach as to *how* to make those special, career-moving, life-changing goals happen once you yourself determine what they could or should be.

This book is intended to get you thinking. Some ideas will be new to you; some presented in a new light. Some are the good old tried-and-true concepts that are hard to ignore and some might seem whacky. But do this - challenge yourself. Look for the things that will help you improve today and set aside the other ideas for another time.

Keep reading even if you find yourself thinking . . .

. . . That's just crazy!

Odds are it probably is! But that's exactly what might be great about it. I invite you to try something a little bit crazy, a little unusual for you. Experiment with the concepts in this book to find the ones that works best for you and your situation.

. . . Great theory, but it would never work in my life.

Really? Are you sure? Read the book with an open mind. At least give all these ideas a chance to develop—a trial run, so to speak. But remember, we are all different with unique experiences, perspectives, personalities and approaches to life and business. Choose those concepts that will work best for you now. Then, revisit all the ideas at another time and see if some of those rejected concepts have a better fit. As they say: "timing is everything... and everything in its time."

. . . Too many concepts—I'll never be able to implement them all.

In essence, that is exactly what this book is about. How do you weed through all the good concepts, solid ideas and obvious solutions so you can focus only on the greatest opportunities? Choose the concepts and techniques that will have the greatest impact on your life and then implement only one or two. Stick to them. Let them improve your life.

And then with your new found time and approach, implement other Peak Performance principles.

This book is not intended to be a textbook on productivity or personal success, but rather a fountain of ideas to stimulate your creativity and imagination, to take advantage of your strengths, and to help you identify those significant tips and techniques that will turn you into a rock star.

HOW TO GET THE MOST OUT OF THIS BOOK

Here are a few ideas on how to make the best use of this book:

► Develop a deep desire to make small, but significant, changes that will enable you to reap the rewards of Peak Performance.

► Use this book every day! Open it once a day—to any page—and read that section. You will be amazed at how any concept can be easily applied to help improve some element of your day. You may not get earth-shattering results every day, but you can be sure that slight improvements will begin to emerge. And within a few weeks you'll be surprised to notice a marked difference in your level of success and satisfaction at work.

► If you can, read each chapter twice before going on to the next one. They're short, but the concepts are deep and important to internalize.

► As you read, stop frequently to ask yourself how you can apply these techniques to improve your own situation.

► Highlight. Underline. Write notes. Make this your 'workbook' of success.... Unless, of course, you've borrowed this copy from a friend — in which case, immediately order your own personal copy.

► Don't ever forget your focus. Take the best three ideas from this book and focus on those until they have been ingrained in your work style and have produced results you can see. Then, and only then, make more adjustments to your life. It's better to do three things right than a hundred things halfway.

This book is filled with stories intended to bring clarity to the principles discussed. Apply these stories to your life. Change the names, modify the circumstances and make them your own. Then you will really connect and be excited to make real changes in how you perform.

SHARE THE WEALTH

I encourage you to share this book and its concepts with your co-workers and other groups within your company. Not only will it make your job easier because people will share your transformative experience in their own ways, but it will also foster a more effective work environment for everyone, including yourself. Share the wealth and succeed together!

Part One

THE WORLD OF PEAK PERFORMANCE

CHAPTER 1
TAKE THE MYSTERY OUT OF SUCCESS

TAKIN' CARE OF BUSINESS
BACHMAN TURNER OVERDRIVE (BTO), 1974

You get up every morning
From your alarm clock's warning
Take the 8:15 into the city
There's a whistle up above
And people pushin', people shovin'
And the girls who try to look pretty

And if your train's on time
You can get to work by nine
And start your slaving job to get your pay
If you ever get annoyed
Look at me I'm self-employed
I love to work at nothing all day

And I'll be...
Taking care of business every day
Taking care of business every way
I've been taking care of business, it's all mine
Taking care of business and working overtime
Work out!

As you climb the ladder of success,
be sure it's leaning against the right building.

—H. Jackson Brown, Jr.

DON'T DO THINGS RIGHT – DO THE RIGHT THINGS

Somewhere along the line, the word "productive" got twisted. Somehow, productive came to mean working harder. "Be more productive," your boss would say, and you'd take that to mean longer days, work through the weekend, take shorter vacations— all those things you dread, that make you unhappy, that prompt you to think "maybe that last job wasn't so bad after all."

But that definition of "productive" doesn't necessarily mean you're going to be "successful." And certainly being productive doesn't mean you have to work harder. Take Suzanne and Henry. One worked harder. The other worked smarter. Which one do you think found success? Read on...

I met both when I graduated college and got a job working at a scientific research company in the public relations department. I worked closely with the marketing group as all of our initiatives were directly linked to the strategies they developed. Suzanne and Henry were two young MBA's hired to create and implement marketing programs to support ten

▶ ───────────────────────────

"Your main goal at work – and the key to self-esteem, self-respect and personal pride – is for you to increasingly develop your personal and corporate effectiveness. The more effective, efficient and productive you are, the better you feel and the more successful you will be. This is a central focus of time power."

—Time Power, by Brian Tracy.

sales offices on the East Coast. Suzanne handled the Northeast and Henry the Southeast. Both started at the same time. Both were given the same resources. They were hired to build innovative marketing campaigns that would uncover new business and help drive regional sales.

Suzanne was a hard worker. She was always first in, arriving at the office before 8:00 a.m. each morning and made an extra effort to take care of as many details as possible. She spent her day immediately responding to e-mails and phone requests, gathering information for all meetings, ensuring that everything she did, down to the smallest detail was done thoroughly and professionally. I really admired her. She seemed like the consummate professional. As bright as she was, Suzanne had little time to develop those major marketing campaigns. But it certainly was through no fault of her own. She barely had a minute to think as she tried to keep up with all the demands of her daily job.

Henry was another matter. He had a different work style. Although he always accomplished those necessary tasks, he made less effort to be consistently thorough on every project. Henry was responsive to most requests, but not immediately. Henry worked hard, but not tirelessly.

Henry's approach was different. He started every day identifying the things he needed to accomplish to meet what he considered his 'real' goals—both intermediate and long-term. He was here to build innovative marketing campaigns and he wanted to spend most of his energies on that objective. Somehow he intuitively knew that his boss would ultimately judge him on how he accomplished that and what he could contribute to the company's success. In other words, Henry knew how to drive his own peak performance.

After a time, Suzanne grew frustrated with her job. No matter how many hours she worked, there were always more things to do on her list (sound familiar?). No matter how much effort she put into every document or report, no one seemed to notice.

To make matters worse, she watched Henry, the co-worker who wasn't even *half* as conscientious as her, get accolades from management and additional responsibilities on the team. She knew she was more capable of creating even better marketing campaigns than Henry— but she was just too busy to get around to doing them.

Turns out Henry got as many e-mails and phone calls every day as Suzanne. But he didn't stop what he was doing on his key projects. He responded to them in batches every two to three hours, making sure to leave no request unfulfilled for more than twenty-four hours. I watched him prioritize the tasks that were asked of him in all these calls and messages, and his response time rarely seemed to be a problem.

Both Suzanne and Henry had the best intentions. Young, energetic, anxious to please, excited at the chances they were given. But while Suzanne was harried all day, every day, Henry's approach was deliberate. Rather than respond to haphazard requests as they happened, Henry prioritized his tasks and activities every day. Both styles were noticed, but only Henry's was noted.

Most important of all, by working smarter, Henry made the time to create several awesome marketing campaigns, which, by the way, got some terrific results! The campaigns got rave reviews in the Southeast region and were ultimately rolled out nationally. Within seven months, Henry was promoted to Manager.

Now, more than twenty years later, Henry is President and CEO of a multinational tool company with revenues exceeding $600 million. He oversees manufacturing facilities on three continents and sells his products in more than twenty countries. Suzanne is Director of Marketing at a small technology company north of Boston.

THE SECRET OF THE PICKLE JAR

These days there are nearly as many theories about leadership and success as there are new apps for the iPhone. But I discovered one that carries the wisdom of the ages, yet still applies to the new world order of today.

It's called the Pickle Jar Theory and I suppose its origins might date back to 1903 when the automatic glass blowing machine was invented and the first pickle jars were produced. (That's a wild guess on my part, but let's go with that for now.) I first heard the story of the Pickle Jar from Larissa Herda, President and CEO of *tw telecom*, when I was an employee of what was then called Time Warner Telecom.

What I love about The Pickle Jar Theory is that it's not just about time management. It's about life balance, work success, and what could ultimately lead to greater personal fulfillment. For this reason, at the core of peak performance, you guessed it, is a pickle jar.

This pickle jar is a powerful metaphor of your business day. Now, if you don't like pickles, fine, because it's not the pickles that are important. It's about the jar. The jar itself represents the time we each have. Everyone has the same pickle jar of time. The big question is how do you choose to fill yours? How do you make the most of that finite time you have been given to be successful each day?

Imagine an empty jar (crispy pickles, succulent peaches, mouth-watering tomatoes, whatever is your fancy) with the contents already eaten. Being empty and clean, you now have the opportunity to fill it - but this time, fill it with four magical ingredients – rocks, pebbles, sand, and water. This isn't an art project, and these are no ordinary rocks, pebbles, sand and water. Each ingredient represents the activities of your day. Allow me to explain.

Rocks are the most important. They represent your top priorities—the most important things you need to accomplish. They are the significant things. They're the stuff that moves you (and your company) forward. In most organizations, these are the activities that typically help generate revenue, support customers or innovate business processes. This might be finalizing a multi-million dollar proposal or creating an innovative marketing strategy to propel the company into a new market. For me, a rock is writing a chapter for my new book or developing a fresh new seminar program. For my publisher, it is editing the book at hand or working on getting new publishing clients. For you, it might be creating a technical support environment to help customers better use the new features of your product or a new pricing structure that makes it easier to purchase your service. Whatever they are, rocks are the most important accomplishments that can move things forward or create positive change.

Rocks are larger and, of course, take up a lot of room in your jar. That means that they are relatively few, but sit high on your priority scale. They also take a lot of time out of your day. They require energy and concentration— and a determination not to let anything get in your way to getting them done. The payoff for fitting as many rocks as possible in your jar is huge. They deliver the greatest possible results for you, which means that rocks can propel you further down your path and make you feel pretty darn good at the end of the day. More on that later.

Next come the pebbles. Because pebbles are a smaller version of rocks, they are closely related. The pebbles represent important activities that support the rocks and help you get the results you want. They might include product research, communicating with the team, brainstorming ideas or developing a format for that big proposal. The pebbles take up less room, but it's guaranteed that there are more of them to get done. The pebbles are often an integral part to moving those rocks forward. The pebbles take up significant room and often cause significant results to happen as well. But remember, they are secondary. They are there to help support the rocks. If they're doing anything else, then they're not pebbles. They're sand.

The sand represents the fun stuff, those things you like to do and make your daily work life enjoyable. The fun stuff might be chatting with or helping your co-workers, planning the company holiday party, checking industry blogs, as well as working on enjoyable tasks that require little effort and take your mind off important, but sometimes stressful things. Unfortunately, these tasks have little impact on the results you're looking for from the rocks.

Finally, there's water. Water represents those things that clutter up your life - things people often perceive as "must-do's" but bring little result or satisfaction. These are the activities that can take up all of your time because they are never ending - things like filing, re-organizing, constantly checking e-mail, attending unimportant meetings and answering phone calls. Too much water happened to drown Suzanne's career because she never fully understood that no matter how much organizing and how many e-mails needed responding, there would always be more.

Henry knew the secret of the Pickle Jar. The secret is this: *Your focus and your time are your most valuable possessions at work.* As Benjamin Franklin once said, "Do you love life? Then do not squander time, for that's the stuff that life is made of." When you invest the majority of your time working on your highest priority tasks, you are getting the most value out of this precious asset. Your work produces results. So consider this: anything you do other than your top priorities is a *relative* waste of time. Let's be fair, though. Sometimes just chatting with a co-worker, while not necessarily "productive" is in fact exactly what you may need at that moment as a little pick-me-up or a way to clear your head. The trick is to use those moments sparingly because a little "tiramisu" (that's *"pick me up"* in Italian) can go a long way.

Let's make it real. Here's a diagram of an ideal jar. Notice that while the rocks are important, they don't dominate. There's a reason for that, which I will share shortly.

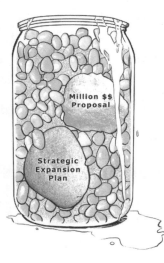

Big Rocks are your priorities: the most important tasks that will move you and your company forward. They are always results oriented activities such as revenue-generating programs, strategic implementation, customer-focused projects – all supporting your organization's mission and goals.

Pebbles are your important tasks: smaller tasks that support your priorities and move you closer to getting results. These can include things like research, planning, analysis, brainstorming, writing, communicating, and professional training – all directly related to your top priorities.

Sand represents your enjoyable tasks: the fun stuff you like to do that is part of your job (and sometimes your personal life), but not critical to your highest priorities. These are things like organizing a department luncheon, work-related blogging and tweeting, assisting co-workers with their projects, updating procedures, customizing standard reports, planning your family vacation – all those things that you like to do, but are not central to your top priorities.

Water is the clutter: the things that are never ending and will never run out; some are a waste of time, others are a natural part of business, but should never become the focal point of your day. These are the endless e-mails, meetings, phone calls, filing, interruptions, paperwork, others' priorities, and office politics. Only add enough water to keep the rest of the jar afloat.

The perfect jar has it all. It is filled with a few big rocks, lots of pebbles, a couple of handfuls of sand and some water to ensure a smooth and efficient integration of all the critical components required for a meaningful day. And if you fill up your jar correctly, your reward is life balance, success at work, and deeper personal happiness. The jar becomes the simple foundation from which star power can emerge.

THE WATER JAR

Now, let's look at how most people fill their jar. They tend to start with the water first; they tend to be like Suzanne. These folks fill up with all those things that clutter their day and never seem to run out.

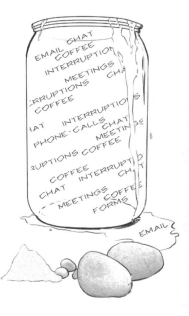

If you start with water first, you have a bit of a problem--you have no room for anything else. You spend your day on meaningless things. At the end of the day, you're tired but have accomplished little of value. No time is left for the million dollar proposal, the strategic plan, competitive research or new product requirements – those things that really matter.

The outcome to a jar full of water is no progress, no results, no way to that ultimate sense of pride and happiness.

THE FUN JAR OF SAND

Then there are those who are always looking for fun, doing the things they like to do instead of doing those things that need to get done. They spend much of their time helping their co-workers, planning family vacation, blogging, reformulating reports, researching themes for the holiday party – doing all those things that make no difference in the larger scheme of things.

They might add some water to eliminate some clutter before the day ends, but they too have no room left for the things that really matter - the million dollar proposal, the strategic plan, competitive research or new product requirements.

At the end of the day, they're very tired, but often feel a little guilty, unfulfilled and most probably frustrated at work.

The outcome of a jar full of sand is no progress, no results and definitely no way to find happiness.

THE PEBBLE PUSHER

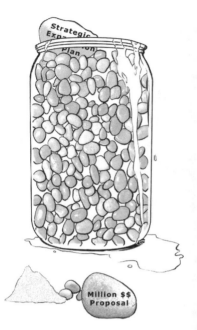

Now, here's a sticky issue. What happens if you fill the jar with pebbles first? I know a lot of people in corporate America who love to do this. They get a lot of important tasks done—research competitive products, train new employees on procedures, attend industry seminars, drive brainstorming meetings, volunteer to compile reports. You get the idea. They often make sure to leave some room for sand (we all like a little fun, after all) and a bit of water, which is unavoidable.

But unfortunately, these pebble-pushers never accomplish any of the priorities that will make the biggest difference in their jobs and for the company. Turns out, they're just, well, pebble pushers. They feel that they've worked especially hard moving all those pebbles around, given it their all. But, they end up wondering what they've accomplished, wondering more about where they are going, and maybe why they are so under-appreciated. Maybe it's because they never got to that million dollar proposal or the strategic plan for the company's future.

The outcome of a jar full of pebbles— some progress, but no results, little advancement and no way to fulfillment and happiness.

THE ROCK STAR'S JAR

And finally, there are the Henrys of the world. They fill the jar with the big rocks first because they know if they do this, they will still have room enough to add those supporting pebbles; and there will still be plenty of space for water and even some sand. These true rock stars will start their day by focusing on their priorities. They will make sure that no matter what, that million dollar proposal will get done and progress will be made on the strategic expansion plan.

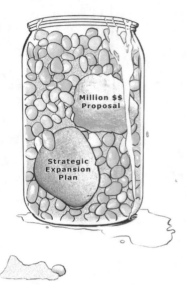

During the day, these professionals clearly understand they will accomplish those important tasks that will move them forward, yield the best results and directly impact their own personal success.

The Henrys of the world know how to achieve their peak performance. Peak performance is really simply filling your pickle jar in the right order. And lo and behold, once you accomplish the important things, everything else simply falls into place. You can then enjoy that fun chat, plan that vacation, take care of those never-ending e-mails... and bask, even briefly, in that satisfying glow of feeling accomplished. In the end, you will be noticed and you will benefit from the sense of accomplishment and pride... and of course all the rewards that come with a job well done.

THE ROAD TO GREATNESS

You control what goes into that jar every single day. Believe this. Unless you truly believe it and internalize it, you will continue to be a victim of other people's whims and priorities.

Fact is you have control of your destiny based on those conscious and subconscious decisions you make each day. You decide whether to let others interrupt - or not; let others make decisions for you - or not; let others use up your time - or not. Accept that even no decision *is* a decision. The sooner you take responsibility for your actions and inactions, the sooner you will be on your way to achieving rock star status.

Your Future is in Your Hands

We're taught from an early age that if we break Mom's favorite dish or hit a baseball through the neighbor's window to "take responsibility." And certainly, responsibility grows from there. As we make decisions about where to attend college, what to study, how to spend our summers and even whom to associate with – our lives take on a unique direction based on all those integrated decisions. Too often, people simply "go along with the flow" and abdicate responsibility to some unknown force.

Responsibility may seem like a burden to some, but life's taught me that it is worth its weight - as exemplified by Liz Murray's story.

Homeless to Harvard

Liz Murray was the daughter of loving, but drug-addicted parents living with a group of like-minded addicts in New York. When Liz was just 15 years old, her mother died of HIV Aids, her father moved into a homeless shelter and Liz was left to make it on her own on the streets of New York City.

Liz was certainly a victim of circumstance and had every right to blame others for her plight. In an interview with Ellie Weiser, she explained "When my mother passed away, I had no place to sleep or eat and every moment was a task in survival." Passing her days with a group of homeless teenagers, most of her time was spent panhandling, hunting for food, socializing, rebel-rousing and surviving. But Liz decided to change her fate. She took responsibility for her life and her future. Liz made the bold decision to go back to high school when most kids her age were graduating.

This real-life Cinderella story was turned into a Lifetime television movie, "Homeless to Harvard: The Liz Murray Story" directed by Peter Levin. The story has a happy ending. Through an essay contest sponsored by the New York Times, Liz earned a scholarship to Harvard University. Although it wasn't an easy road, Liz completed her studies and graduated Harvard with a degree in psychology in June, 2009.

Rather than continue to be a victim of circumstance, Liz became a creator of circumstance. She took responsibility for her future, control of her life and achieved success.

WHY THE CEO LIKES HIS JOB

There's something really interesting about responsibility. An essential part of being successful is taking 100 percent responsibility for things you can affect in your life - your successes, your failures, your relationships, your health, everything, including your daily routines and actions.

No one is saying it's easy to do this. Most of us have been conditioned to blame outside influences for those things in life we don't like. We blame our parents, our boss, our teachers, our friends, co-workers, spouses, the weather, the economy, the car, the tennis racquet—anything or anyone we can pin with the blame. For some reason it's much easier to blame others than to take responsibility and blame ourselves. But there's a price you pay when you do that. You give up control. And that's part of what we're talking about here, regaining control.

There is good news here. With responsibility comes control. And with control comes so much more. That's why most CEOs love being CEOs. Sure they might take the fall if the company performs poorly, but they relish having full control to build it the way they want to build it, to be completely responsible for that . . . and to ultimately reap the glory that comes with rock star status!

Dr. Seuss tried to introduce us to this concept at a very young age. He wrote:

> *You have brains in your head.*
> *You have feet in your shoes.*
> *You can steer yourself in any direction you choose.*
> *You're on your own. And you know what you know.*
> *You are the guy who'll decide where to go.*

> —*Oh! The Places You'll Go, by Dr. Seuss*

"It has come to my attention that you are taking performance enhancing drugs. Keep up the good work."

CHAPTER 2
KNOWING WHAT YOU WANT IS HARD...
GETTING IT IS EASY

I WANT IT ALL
QUEEN, 1989

I want it all
I want it all
I want it all and I want it now

I'm a man with a one track mind
So much to do in one lifetime
Not a man for compromise and where's and why's and living lies
So I'm living it all, yes I'm living it all
And I'm giving it all, and I'm giving it all
I want it all

If you don't work towards achieving your own goals, you are destined to work towards achieving the goals of others.
—Someone wise and Anonymous

A FOUNDATION MADE OF ROCKS

Going after success is a top down affair. Richard Carlson wrote the book, *Don't Sweat the Small Stuff.* He was right — as long as you know what the big stuff is. So let's get this party started by focusing on the big stuff in your jar, the rocks, the ultimate goals you want to accomplish.

The most common time waster and biggest obstacle to success in life is losing sight of what you are trying to accomplish, or simply forgetting what you set out to do. Many people work hard every day but they have no clear idea of their real goals and objectives.

So the first thing you need to know about rocks — or rather goals — is you need to actually have them! How many of you can list, with clarity, the immediate goals that you need to accomplish at work? Do it and time yourself. If you're taking longer than, say, thirty seconds, you definitely need to pay attention to what I'm about to say.

Without the shadow of a doubt, you must have your goals at work clearly defined, because if you don't, then you can't start with the right combination of ingredients to create that perfect recipe for success and ultimate career satisfaction. An interesting side benefit here — there's something amazing about this goal-setting concept. If you get it all together at work with the right goals being set, then even those big life goals become that much more attainable... and life becomes a whole lot more satisfying.

WHAT DO HARVARD, ARNOLD AND A PENCIL HAVE IN COMMON?

Your work goals should not be that difficult to figure out; they're usually defined by your company's, your department's or your team's overall mission and goals as identified by top management. Your job now is to clarify those goals and write them down. This is so important, I have to repeat it. Your job is to clarify those goals and write them down. Writing them down is one of the most critical elements to actually achieving your goals.

Think I'm nuts? Let me give you a famous example of a goal study that was done in 1979. Mark McCormack, one of the most successful entrepreneurs and author of *What They Don't Teach You at Harvard Business School,* decided to explore the validity of setting goals. He wanted to answer the questions: Do goals really make a difference? Does setting goals really matter?

McCormack approached the 1979 graduating class at Harvard Business School and asked them a simple question: "Have you set clear, written goals for your future and made plans to accomplish them?" The responses were classic.

Three percent of the graduates had written goals and plans. Thirteen percent had goals, but they were not in writing. And 84 percent had no specific goals at all. Presumably, this final group of bright young people had the goal of graduating with a Harvard MBA; and then armed with that precious diploma, they'd simply follow the path of one of the many excellent opportunities that would be placed before them.

Ten Years Later

Ten year later, Mark McCormack followed up with these graduates and this is what he discovered: The thirteen percent of the class that had goals were earning *two* times as much as the 84 percent who had no goals at all. That is quite impressive. However, what is really astounding is that the three percent, who had written goals, were earning, on average, ten times as much as the other 97 percent. *Wow!* Now I don't know what else was going on with those three percenters, but I do know this, when you write your goals down in black and white that puts conviction behind them. That gives those goals tremendous power.

"Your mind is remarkable," writes Jack Canfield in his book, *The Success Principles.* "Something amazing happens between your head and your fingers. The very act of writing out your goal clearly means that you have the ability to achieve it somehow. Your desire is the only real limit on your potential."

Hasta La Vista, Baby

Hollywood is really the land of overachievers, if you think about it, and there are a ton of stories about how actors make impossible goals and then make them come true. My favorite has to do with the Governator. Yes, Arnold Schwarzenegger.

When the young "Ahhnold" was ten years old, living in a small village in Austria, he had the dream of coming to America. One of six children in a modest home, it seemed an unlikely dream, so Arnold created a plan. He was confident that if he could become a great bodybuilder and win the Mr. Universe competition, that would be his ticket to the United States.

With that goal in mind, Arnold started lifting weights seriously when he was fifteen years old and ultimately became the youngest ever Mr. Universe at the age of twenty. His success grew and he went on to win the most prestigious Mr. Olympia competition (contest between all the Mr. Universe winners) an unprecedented seven years in a row.

As a result of his bodybuilding success, Arnold was featured in a documentary called *Pumping Iron* (1977). Surprising everyone at the end of the filming, Arnold announced that he would be retiring from professional bodybuilding. The astonished producer asked: "So what's next for you?" And Arnold simply responded: "I have been the best bodybuilder in the world. Now I am going to Hollywood to be the best actor in the world."

You can almost hear the chuckle coming from behind the camera and imagine the producer's thoughts: Hollywood? You've got to be kidding. You've got muscles for brains. You have no formal education. You barely speak English and people can't even pronounce your name. You're going to Hollywood to become a great actor? Now that's funny.

But Arnold wasn't laughing. He may not have known exactly how he was going to get there—and I doubt he had any political aspirations at the time—but he had absolute clarity about where he was going and what he wanted to achieve.

And that's the next thing about goals you need to know. They need to be clear, no matter how farfetched they may seem.

Now I think you get the point that peak performance— the Secret of the Jar, as I've been calling it—is built on the principle that if you focus on the important things, the rocks in your jar, you are setting yourself up to achieve your true breakthrough goals and ultimate success.

But how does one do this?

DREAM IT. DO IT. LIVE IT.

To determine what is really important, you must be crystal clear about your goals and objectives. Clearly defining your goals and then working with single-minded focus on the most important things you can possibly to do achieve them is the secret to victory.

Master the Skill of Success

Some have called goal setting the "master skill of success." While "master skill" sounds a bit over the top, your ability to clearly set goals and make the plans for their accomplishment will help you achieve success and happiness more than any other skill you can develop.

"Where There's a Will There's a Win." This is the title of a chapter in Donald Trump's book, *Trump 101*. According to The Donald, "Positive thinking isn't always enough. In addition to being positive, you must also be persistent. Being positive and persistent are inseparable – like success and me." It would be nice to have Donald Trump's confidence— and success— so there's a good lesson here.

To make that pickle jar work for you, to get those results you want that are going to make you and your boss happy, more than anything else it requires you to plan and organize your life in such a way that you accomplish your most important goals *as quickly as possible* and then continue on with grander goals and bigger accomplishments. But first, you must know deep in your heart and clear in your mind, your end game – exactly what you want to see happen. Without clarity, your path will be undefined and your end result will likely be disappointing. It's almost impossible to feel satisfied when you don't know what you're striving for. It's simple. Decide precisely what you want and then go get it. Those rocks will allow you to achieve great success.

Let me give you some examples of what I'm talking about:

Bad rock *(murky, ineffective goal):* I want to increase my sales so that I can earn more money next year.

Good rock *(clear, motivating goal):* I want to achieve $15.5 million in sales by December 30th so that I can earn $350,000 next year.

Bad rock *(murky, ineffective goal):* I want to introduce our new product through live customer seminars in our largest cities.

Good rock *(clear, motivating goal):* I plan to develop a five-city product introduction seminar tour with at least 100 attendees, in our five largest revenue-producing markets in the first quarter.

See the difference? The first goal is what you may generally want, but it's not specific enough to drive a strategy or even get you excited about creating one. Without specifics, there's no way to plan and create a clear path or even evaluate how you're progressing towards your goal.

A quality goal will make you a STAR. Although there are many acronyms that have been used to define and develop successful goals, I've created this one in keeping with becoming a Rock Star. The concepts that create a Rock STAR goal are critical to your success:

S – State it in writing

T – Time-specific

A – Actionable

R – Results

Each component is critical to the goal's success. Since I've already made my point about writing the goal down, I'm not going to say anything more—except that you need to **state it in writing.**

A goal must be **time-specific.** Above I mentioned that you want to achieve your goal quickly, so you can continue to achieve bigger things and greater goals. What if you had a goal of reaching a million dollars in sales? If you don't put down a specific date, it may take you thirty years to make those million bucks. Now if I remember my decimal points right, one million divided by thirty is $33,333. So you gross an extra $33,333 in sales every year. You think not bad, but you forget. You only get 10 percent in commission, so you've actually earned $3,333.30 annually. Hmm, after taxes, that may get you a weekend getaway at the beach. Not what you had in mind when you envisioned that million dollar goal was it? So when you're writing your goals down, think about this: by what date do you need to achieve the results in order to make the greatest impact? This week? Next month? Next year? Without a deadline, you cannot monitor your progress and you will have little motivation to move this goal forward.

Your goal must be **actionable**. Actionable means that you have the ability to act upon it. Think of it this way: if all of this is about making good choices and being in control of your life, then you have the choice to act or not to act. If you are unable to take action and make your goal happen, or if the goal you wrote down is "out of your control," then don't waste your time. Find a goal that you can control. For example, if you run the marketing department, you can work towards the goal: "To generate 10,000 sales leads per quarter," but you cannot commit to a goal that states: "To close 250 sales per quarter." That goal rests upon the effectiveness of the sales team – a group you have no control over. Or, as director of technical support, you can develop a goal: "To respond to customer e-mail support requests within two hours of receipt," but you cannot take responsibility "to deliver a product without technical glitches" since you don't control the quality of the product that is developed by the product team. Be sure your goal is one you can take action on and control; otherwise, it's a waste of time and effort to try.

Finally, the next letter, R, assures no misunderstanding. What are the exact **results** required to achieve success. Look back at the examples I just gave you. The first one in each example is vague. The second one has definable deliverables that can be measured. You must state in your goal exactly what you are trying to achieve in concrete terms. If your desire is to increase sales, your goal must state exactly how much you want to increase your sales by. If your goal is decrease costs, you must state by exactly how much you want costs lowered. If you goal is to reduce turnover, you must define a measurement by which you can measure results. And here's the neat thing. A measurement allows you to track your success; to make sure you're on target and if not, figure out what you can do to get back on track. Managing yourself to success, that's what it's all about.

Here are some more examples of effective and ineffective goals so you get the feel for developing a STAR quality goal:

INEFFECTIVE GOAL	EFFECTIVE GOAL
Develop product training for new employees.	Develop a two-day product training class for new employees by March 31.
Decrease production costs this quarter	Limit production costs to $53 per unit for all product manufactured in the first quarter.
Improve employee turnover problem	Maintain employee turnover below 8 percent in 2010.
Workout more to get in better shape.	Work out three times every week to reach 20 percent body fat by September 30, 2010.
Lose weight before my vacation.	Lose 15 pounds by May 1, 2010.

Goals Achieved Great Success in this Atlanta Company

And just in case you think these studies are anomalies and that this STAR goal stuff applies only to those elite who have the privilege of attending Harvard Business School think again. Here is what I personally experienced with one of my clients, a telecommunications company in Atlanta, Georgia.

Due to economic ups and downs, this sales office had been inactive for quite a few years and was now slated to be completely overhauled. This could have been a bad thing with people being demoted or worse, losing their jobs. At that time, when compared by profitability to the other offices around the company's network, the Atlanta office consistently ranked in the bottom 20 percent of the eighty-four markets where this company offered its services.

To turn this city's sales operations around, the company hired an aggressive and creative General Manager to come in, develop the market and grow the city. Rick came with more than twenty years of sales and business experience to help Atlanta realize the kind of sales revenue a city like that was able to achieve. Rick hired professionals in sales, technical support, operations, administration and management. He was a big believer in goals and every week, at their Monday morning team meetings, Rick asked each person to write down their five goals for the week. Those goals included three work related goals and two personal goals. So a salesperson's weekly goal list might include:

1. Make twenty-five phone calls to prospects (work)
2. Deliver five new sales proposals (work)
3. Have three new customer meetings (work)
4. Work out three times (personal)
5. Leave work by 4:45 p.m. on Thursday to attend my daughter's soccer game (personal)

Rick asked each person if they would be willing to post their goals on the outside of their cube walls. Most did. And this became the culture of the Atlanta office.

When I visited this city, I would walk between the cubes and see the goals posted on the walls. I could hear the friendly banter: Have you made your twenty-five phone calls this week? Who won your daughter's soccer game yesterday? How are those proposals going? It was truly fun to watch everyone being everyone else's cheerleader.

As the year progressed, Atlanta's profitability rose as did their ranking on the company's monthly sales listing. Atlanta is a wonderful business market and everyone expected excellent growth, but no one expected the incredible growth that was achieved in the next nine months.

By the end of the fiscal year, the Atlanta market was beginning to consistently rank at the top end of the spectrum. They had achieved phenomenal growth and were garnering the attention of top management. At the annual General Managers Meeting in Denver, many of the executives approached Rick and asked: How did you do it? How did you achieve such impressive growth in such a short period of time?

Rick's response was simple. "I am a believer of goals. Every week everyone in my office wrote down their goals for the week. Every day every single person knew exactly what they were planning to accomplish. Although we may not have always reached our goals, we always knew exactly what we were striving for."

By the way, today Rick is Vice President of the entire western region.

New Year's Resolutions

USA today wrote an article, in February 2003, about New Year's resolutions. One year earlier, the newspaper had interviewed people about their resolutions in 2002 and divided the respondents into two categories: those who had written down their resolutions and those who had just thought about them. What they discovered one year later was that only four percent of the people who had made resolutions but did not write them down, had made any changes. On the other hand, 46 percent of those who had written down their resolutions had actually followed through on them and made changes in their lives. The simple act of writing it down made the difference between triumph and defeat.

"It wasn't an easy decision for me to make.
Lots of coin tossing went into it."

CHAPTER 3
ACTIONS SPEAK LOUDER THAN WORDS

BREAK ON THROUGH (TO THE OTHER SIDE)
THE DOORS, 1966

Made the scene week to week,
Day to day, hour to hour,
The gate is straight, deep and wide,
Break on through to the other side,
Break on through to the other side,
Break on through,
Break on through,
Break on through,
Break on through,
Break, break, break, break,
Break, break, break, break,
Break.

After all is said and done,
a lot more will have been said than done.

—Author Unknown

JUST DO IT . . . AND DON'T STOP!

Goals are powerful. Goals are a simple solution to getting the results you want. All you have to do is make them happen. Easier said than done, right?

The STAR formula alleviates some of the confusion about actually creating goals that work. But there's something else about goals that you may not know. And this is the trick that turns your goals into those golden rocks of results that put you on the road to rock star status. The basic concept is this: you've set your goal. Now what you have to do is figure out the way in which you're going to go about achieving that goal. Visualization is good, but it won't make your goal a reality. What are the actual steps you need to take, the things you need to do, the actions you need to accomplish, to make that goal happen?

Goals can only be reached by practical action. "It is no use imagining that you will be able to drive a car if you simply read the manual or study the rules of the road. You cannot learn to dance, paint or cook by perusing texts or recipes," writes Karen Armstrong in *A Case for God*. "There are some things that can be learned (or achieved) only by constant, dedicated practice; but if you persevere, you find that you (can) achieve something that seemed initially impossible."

At work and in life, you need to have your goals, and you need to have a clear plan of action in order to make them happen. Once you set the process in motion, you create energy and a momentum that will drive you forward. Here's how:

Decide where you're going

I can't stress this point enough (as you can tell). Crystallize what you are trying to achieve and by when—that puts you squarely on the right path.

Create Your Strategy

The original meaning of the word strategy is derived from the Greek *strategia*, which is often used in military terms and represents the ability to employ available resources to win a war. That's a powerful metaphor. All too often, to get to that ultimate goal, it takes a hard-fought battle, using all your resources and personal stamina to get there. There is no getting around it - you need a good strategy to be successful.

Strategy is the GPS of the 21st century; outlining your chosen path or a general direction to start you on your way. Think about it. How are you planning to get to the top of the mountain? Will you take the snake path or climb straight up. Will you blaze a new trail or take advantage of the existing terrain?

A solid strategy is the foundation of successful execution and completion. Too many people have derailed their own efforts by jumping right into tactics and implementation without first developing a coherent strategy. Those who have been most successful have taken the time to develop a quality plan that is aligned with their ultimate goals and personal motivations.

There is no magic formula for developing a valid strategy and there are many strategic possibilities for every goal. The key is to create a strategy that ensures you keep your eye on the prize. A strategy must be consistent with your skills, values and resources; and continually move you in the right direction. Do not allow your strategy to get off track, to be diverted by others' priorities or to lose momentum. Your strategy is the basis of your tactical implementation, the fundamental element of ultimate success.

Take Action

Action is what it takes to get there. If the ultimate goal is winning the war, actions are your battle march. Ah, this is where *actionable* becomes real, where every strategy is supported by tactical steps propelling you to your destination.

Sometimes our greatest goals seem overwhelming, too big to realistically accomplish; but in reality, goals are just a series of small tasks. If you break down your goal into all the manageable tasks and activities that are needed to get you there, it becomes much more attainable. Bite sizes pieces are much easier to swallow and before you know it, you will have your just dessert!

The trick to making this work is that you need to write down every task required. They are your pebbles, the things that must get done in order to finally achieve your goals. The beauty of having this list, no matter how long or daunting it may seem, is that it defines your path to realizing your goals, your ultimate success and happiness.

▶ ────────────────────────────

Example: Plan to accomplish your goal

Decide Where You're Going:
Publish a book that teaches professionals the secrets of developing a personal philosophy of Peak Performance by December 31.

Develop the Strategy:
Base the book on the seminars, workshops and presentations I have made on this topic to over 1,000 professionals. Use

materials I developed for these programs as well as lessons I learned from the attendees' feedback and also my 30 years of professional experience.

Take Action

► Develop the central theme and concept of the book
► Create an outline of general topics of discussion – the initial Table of Contents
► Develop content ideas for each section
► Identify key points that will drive the message
► Find and create stories that clarify each idea
► Review all past presentation materials and highlight key topic areas that can be applied to the book
► Read all program feedback forms and collect new material developed during the seminars and workshops
► Write opening introduction that includes central theme and point of book
► Identify a mastermind group that can be my reality check on concepts and ideas I develop and include – people who will give candid feedback and good advice
► Create a timeline based on the Table of Contents to use as guideline for accomplishment
► Research and interview editors
► Research and interview book designers
► Develop marketing strategy
► Write, write, write...
► And so on...

BREAK THROUGH TO HIGHER GROUND

Although setting goals is an excellent start, the process of setting goals provides us with a unique opportunity if we approach it the right way. Typically, we tend to think of goals more in the short term than with an eye towards the longer range future. We create simple goals. *Finish that proposal. Close three new accounts this month. Finalize the annual budget. Clean out the basement. Lose 10 pounds.* We think about the now perhaps, instead of the future. We think small steps instead of giant leaps.

In life, if you don't think big, you will never get big. Only big goals will have a big impact on your life, your future and your success. Donald Trump says: "If you're going to be thinking, you might as well think big. Thinking big can get you to the top."

Think about your goals for the next five years. Is there one goal which would be a breakthrough goal? That is, the goal that, if achieved, would create a huge shift in your life or career? What could that goal possibly be that would seriously up-level everything, from your income to your opportunities to your lifestyle?

Too Much or Not Enough?

When I started my first sales job, the Vice President of our division visited our sales training class to talk about setting goals. Sales are all about goals, he said, otherwise known as your quota. It's also about earning potential. Everyone knows that the best sales people earn the most money.

Our VP told us a story about how he started setting his goals. In his first year of sales, he decided on a personal goal and posted it on the mirror in his bathroom at home. When his wife saw his goal she said: "I have full confidence in you, honey, but don't you think you should set a goal that is more realistic?" Although he was taken aback, he simply replied: "This is my goal and I will work hard to achieve it."

At the end of the year, he achieved his goal. With much pride and fanfare he posted a new, bigger goal for the following year. His wife looked at it and said: "You achieved great success last year, and I'm impressed with your ability and confidence, but don't you think this one is really overly ambitious?" Yet again he replied: "Absolutely not. This is my goal and I plan to achieve it."

Once again, he achieved his goal. He proceeded to put next year's goal on his bathroom mirror. This time when his wife looked at what he wrote, she said point blank: "Seriously, that's all?"

In my workshops I talk about the importance of having breakthrough goals. These are the goals that can take your career and often your life, to the next level. They are those things that seem to be an incredible stretch, but they're not, in fact, unrealistic.

Here is an example. What if you were a young entrepreneur building a start-up business and were able to win your industry's *Entrepreneur of the Year* award. How would achieving that goal change your life? Possibly these are some of the things that might happen as a result:

► Your business would be recognized as innovative and reliable by professionals in your industry, attracting new prospects.
► You would attract new and bigger opportunities than ever before.
► Large established companies would feel more comfortable doing business with you.
► You would find it easier to partner with other industry leaders.
► Investors would become aware of you and your company and explore ways to get involved with your growth and expansion.
► Your income would increase dramatically.
► Your business could grow at an even faster pace.

▶ You would achieve wonderfully valuable recognition and great personal pride.

All this from a single breakthrough goal.

Will this happen overnight? No! But it will happen with perseverance, relentless effort and ongoing focus one day at a time until you achieve your goal.

THE RULE OF ONE

One of the reasons people fail at goals is that they look at what they dream of accomplishing and they become overwhelmed. But if, when looking at your lofty goal, you take a step back, you will realize that accomplishing anything significant in life requires something simple and basic. It requires simply making whatever progress is possible, however slight, by unrelentingly and consistently taking some action. Remember – a house is built one brick at a time. Football games are won one play at a time. Dreams are achieved one goal at a time. Goals are achieved one action at a time.

In the end, every goal-setting exercise must be reduced to specific, concrete action steps that you can take to achieve that goal. Create your action list and set realistic deadlines for each one. And above all else, always apply the Rule of One. I like this rule because it makes everything doable. You don't have to do twenty things; you just do what's next!

The Rule of One states: take *one* action, large or small, *every* day towards achieving your goal. That adds up to five things focused on achieving your goal every week, twenty things every month, sixty actions every quarter. Imagine the enormous progress you will make towards achieving your breakthrough goal. I know you'll agree that it's more than worth it.

No matter how far away the goal may seem, every single action will keep you motivated and focused. Daily movement towards achieving your goal will be energizing and increase your confidence that no matter how big you dream, you are in control and it's you who is making it happen.

When you do something every day that moves you closer to your goal, you will develop an unshakable belief that your goal will ultimately be achieved. And it will.

CHAPTER 4
MAN DOES NOT LIVE BY
ROCKS AND PEBBLES ALONE

GOOD TIME
ALAN JACKSON, 2008

Work, *work all week long*
Punchin' that clock from dusk till dawn.
Countin' the days till Friday night
That's when all the conditions are right.
For a good time
I need a good time.

All work and no play makes Jack a dull boy.

—Old Proverb

SOME DISTRACTIONS ARE GOOD DISTRACTIONS

Jack needs some down time to enjoy himself and the world around him. That's why even the sand and water are important elements of the peak performance pickle jar.

Setting goals and taking action to actually make them a reality are your rocks and pebbles. These tasks and activities are the key to getting you where you want to go. But man does not live by rocks and pebbles alone. That's why you must mix in and make the time for sand and water every day. After all, in the world of pickle jars, that's what all those nooks and crannies are for.

Allow me to first elaborate on sand, because that's the fun stuff. It might be composing that perfect spreadsheet, sending routine e-mail, chatting with co-workers, working on low priority projects you enjoy, planning your daughter's birthday party or simply taking a walk. There are hundreds of ways we choose to be distracted during the day. In fact, these distractions, in small doses, are healthy and a natural part of life; and frankly necessary. Nevertheless, beware the danger of too many distractions. Distractions, like chocolate and ice cream, are fine in moderation. But too much will slow you down.

It's true. In order to manage your time effectively you need to make room for fun and entertainment. There's only one problem, much of the fun stuff can be addicting. It feeds procrastination, and there's a fine line between pouring a little sand in between the rocks and pebbles, and spending the entire afternoon shopping online.

Many of my clients have told me that they lose track of time when they're surfing the internet, catching up with office gossip or customizing that perfect slide presentation. Before they know it, five minutes has turned into thirty minutes, an hour, or more. Next thing you know, it's 5:00 p.m. and you haven't even started on the client proposal, which is due this week. The proposal (a big rock obviously) is not something you want to rush through, let alone forget. Do yourself a favor and don't create a personal dilemma by indulging in too much sand. Hanging out on your own private beach in your office will seriously crimp your ability to do the things that will make a real difference to your ultimate success. Stay on the program. Moving those significant things forward may give you just as much enjoyment and ultimately so much more to feel good about.

Focus. Focus. Focus.
There's room for sand in the jar, but be careful when you add it in. If you take care to focus first on the rock and pebbles, then by all means, have at it. Make that special time to fill in with some meaningful sand and enjoy every moment of it.

As the proverb states: All work and no play makes Jack a dull Boy. On the other hand: "All play and no work makes Jack a mere toy."

Clutter drains your energy
and you never realize it until it's gone.
—New Proverb

OTHER DISTRACTIONS WILL DROWN YOU

So what about water? Water is the stuff in your jar that you don't want to deal with, the clutter in your life that seems to never run out.

Guess what? No matter how far into the sand you stick your head, you will always have more papers to file, forms to fill out, e-mails to read, stuff to put away, lists to reorganize, useless meetings to attend, and nonsense phone calls to answer. That's the real world, and we all have to face up to it.

But… not all water is created equal—and that holds true for the water in your jar.

There's the necessary water and the really nasty water. To some it may be a matter of perspective, but the endless stream of papers, e-mails, meetings, anything that threatens to clutter your day may also be an integral part of your day. And here's the kicker—just as sand can suffocate the hours you have available for work, so can water drown you in its never-ending stream.

So, like all things in life, moderation is key. Imagine filling your pickle jar first with water, the clutter. The tap will continue to pour until your jar is overflowing. You will become run down simply trying to stay afloat. You must never sacrifice important tasks for these water activities. They will drain you of time, productivity and all your energy. You will be left exhausted with little to show for your efforts. But you must also learn to manage them so that they don't drown you through sheer neglect, either.

Think of your jar as a thriving metaphor of your life. And as such, you need to water it every day. Keep up with your e-mail, respond to your phone calls, file your papers, and organize your desk. As long as you allow some time for this on a daily basis, the clutter will not overrun your priorities or soak up your sand.

The trick is to keep the clutter under control instead of letting the clutter control you. This means responding to e-mail in chunks, letting phone calls go to voicemail until you find the time to talk and organizing your files only after you have finished your priority tasks. Water shouldn't soak up your *prime time*, but rather fill in the gaps of your *down time*.

And, just as water is necessary to life, consistently taking care of the clutter will give you peace of mind and the ability to clearly see the bigger picture and the opportunities that lay ahead.

"IT'S NOT ALL FUN AND GAMES, ALTHOUGH I'LL ADMIT IT'S MOSTLY FUN AND GAMES."

Part Two

YOU AND PEAK PERFORMANCE

CHAPTER 5
FOCUS. FOCUS. AND FOCUS.

TIME
PINK FLOYD, 1973

Ticking away the moments that make up a dull day
You fritter and waste the hours in an offhand way.
Kicking around on a piece of ground in your home town
Waiting for someone or something to show you the way.

Tired of lying in the sunshine staying home to watch the rain.
You are young and life is long and there is time to kill today.
And then one day you find ten years have got behind you.
No one told you when to run, you missed the starting gun.

A fool with a plan can outsmart
a genius with no plan any day.

—T. Boone Pickens: Boonism #29

YOU BETTER HAVE A PLAN

Dapper Danny Ocean, the lead character in the movie series *Ocean's 11*, is a man with a very big plan. Less than twenty-four hours into his parole from a New Jersey penitentiary, the charismatic thief is already rolling out his next plan. In one night, Danny and his ten-man crew of specialists steal over $150 million from three Las Vegas casinos owned by a ruthless entrepreneur who happens to be dating Danny's ex-wife. The entire movie focuses on Danny's elaborate plan and orchestrating it to perfection – pulling off the most daring heist in the history of Las Vegas. It's not easy. The plan requires pick-pocketing, demolition, technological mastery and daring acrobatics. But solid planning pays off as the team rides away with $150 million. And if that wasn't enough, Danny even gets the girl. Amazing what a good plan (and a nice Hollywood budget) will get you.

Most plans are not as elaborate, don't require such a diverse set of skills, and don't result in a $150 million payout. But all successful ventures have a plan and all plans do require follow through. Danny Ocean had to have a plan in place in order to pull off the heist, but he also knew that if any one of the "specialists" on his team did not follow through on their part of the plan, the ultimate goal would never happen.

How do you put a plan in place so it actually has a chance of success? Read on.

Get Focused and Stay Focused

Plans get you focused. Period. They make up the pebbles that support your rocks. Your plan leads you into action and moves you towards the results you want. *Your* plan ... *your* results; these are the key concepts. You must create your own plan; otherwise, you will succumb to the demands and plans of others.

▶━━━━━━━━━━━━━━━━━━━━━━━━━━━━━━━━━━━━━

The most important thing about a plan is simply having one.

━━━━━━━━━━━━━━━━━━━━━━━━━━━━━━━━━━━━━━

The first thing to understand about a good plan is that it must reflect your most important goals and objectives, which are then prioritized by timing, impact or value. Depending on your organization, your own job, and the specific needs of your team, your ultimate business goal may be a reflection of a variety of objectives:

▶ Sales Growth and Revenue Expectations
▶ Customer Requirements and Needs
▶ Product Innovation
▶ Competitive or Economic Pressures
▶ Market Opportunities
▶ Government Regulations
...Feel free to add to this list...

This list may or may not help you. If you really don't know what to focus on, and you're not sure of your objectives, maybe the following concepts will help. In his book, *Time Power*, Brian Tracy suggests you ask yourself these questions:

▶ Why am I on the payroll?
▶ What have I been hired to accomplish?
▶ What is my major goal or objective right now?
▶ What am I supposed to be doing at this moment?
▶ What results have I been hired to achieve?
▶ Is what I am doing right now contributing to my most important goals?

WHAT DOES YOUR CEO WANT?

Ultimately, in order to be perceived as successful at work, you should be working on what your boss considers the most important tasks and projects.

When asked what specific qualities would help a young person advance fastest in their career, over 80 percent of CEOs agreed on the top two qualities: (1) the ability to "separate the relevant from the irrelevant"; that is, focus on those tasks that really matter to the company, and (2) the ability to "get the job done fast." Make it happen. Get it done. Take 100% responsibility to make things happen.

It really is all about figuring out the relevant over the irrelevant. When you can separate the two and get the job done efficiently, your career moves into the fast lane. When you are accomplishing your company's highest priorities, trust me on this, you will be noticed.

Every day, as you decide what tasks to complete, what work to prioritize and what projects to delegate, consider your objective first, and then ensure that your energy is focused on activities that will support that objective. Spend most of your time working on the one objective that will make the greatest impact. In the end, you will have real results to show. And frankly isn't that all that really matters?

▶ ━━

The Woodpecker

A woodpecker can tap twenty times on a thousand trees and get nowhere, but stay very busy. Or, he can tap twenty thousand times on one tree and get dinner.

Be sure to stay focused....otherwise, you will go hungry!

NOT EVERYTHING'S A PRIORITY

Too often, too many things on our plate appear to be priorities. When asked to prioritize, I've actually had clients tell me that "everything is a priority." This is simply not so. To simplify the issue of prioritizing, remember that in business, it's usually all about the money. If what you are working on is either making money for your company or saving money for your company, it's important. Using this basic concept may help you prioritize your activities every day.

Of course, not everything you do directly makes or saves the company money, but many of your activities support these ultimate goals. Every company is built around either delivering a service or selling a product. Depending on your job within the organization, the activities you do help make it happen. You are judged and valued by your ability to influence these fundamental aspects of your company's business.

Go back and look at your major tasks. How close are they aligned to the core of your business? How many steps removed are you from the core fundamentals? The answer to this question is the key to your priorities. Never stray too far from the revenue line.

For example: If your company is a box manufacturer and you are the marketing manager, you might look at your activities as follows, and do them in the following order:

Closest to the revenue: Coordinate details of annual trade show where company sells product on the show floor and identifies new customers. *(Do this first.)*

Closer to revenue: Respond to partner request for marketing materials. *(Help partners bring sales and revenue to company.)*

Close to revenue: Work with printer to print new product brochures; ensure quality is good and price is reasonable. (*Save the company money.*)

Not so close to revenue: Clean out supply closet *(Do this last.)* Donald Trump fired an entire competitive team, named the Excel Team, on his reality TV show, *The Apprentice,* because they took their eyes off the real goal and lost their focus. In one episode, two teams were challenged to create a compelling attraction that would bring shoppers into a sports equipment store for the purpose of increasing sales.

The Excel team was very creative. They developed a remarkable family activity that shoppers loved so much that they spent all their time at the batting cages (their creative idea to attract customers into the store) and didn't buy product. Although the Excel Team created the more popular attraction, what good did it do? It didn't increase sales. In fact, store sales decreased because shoppers were too distracted by the fun activity. Excel completely lost sight of their goal. They worked hard, created a successful event, but failed miserably at the ultimate goal to increase revenue.

OH NO! IT'S FIVE ALREADY?

Most of us know that it's important to start with a plan. But here's a very typical scenario. With the best of intentions you head to work with a plan and a definite idea of what you would like to accomplish today. You set your mind on one task and promise yourself that as soon as you arrive at the office, you will get a quick cup of coffee, keep morning pleasantries to a minimum and then focus on your plan, accomplishing your one priority. As you begin working, your co-workers arrive and the day takes on its usual trappings of interruptions, phone calls, emergencies, conversations, meetings, etc. Somehow, you get involved in several other "priorities," and before you know it, the day is half gone and you have not accomplished, or even started on, your own plan or your own priorities.

How familiar does that sound? When asked "what happened?" Most people reply: "I just didn't have the time. Too many pressing issues." Sorry, but wrong answer! The concept of not having enough time to do the things you "should" do is false and will continue to make your life miserable until you recognize the fact that *you always have enough time!* It's your use of time that will determine what you get done. On busy days, the time you had available to devote to specific tasks was always there. You simply chose to use that time for something else. That was your call.

Let's say you decide to accomplish two key priorities today: complete your quarterly budget and write a letter of introduction to a new customer. Among everything on your plate, those are two things you want to be sure to accomplish today. That's your general plan for the day. The time to complete these two tasks will probably be one-and-a-half hours. You arrive at work at 8:30 and usually leave at about 5:30. You have plenty of time. How you choose to spend it is the real issue here.

As usual, you start your day by answering e-mails, returning phone calls, meeting with people who drop by your office, attending scheduled and unscheduled meetings, chatting with co-workers, reviewing random documents, returning more phone calls, checking and responding to more e-mails, providing unsolicited feedback on the new trade show booth, going out to lunch, running a few errands, checking e-mail, returning phone calls....Oops, it's 5:00 o'clock. Better start to wrap up the day.

Did you have the time to take care of those two key priorities? Of course you did. But you allowed yourself to get distracted by low priority items that gobbled up your time and energy all day long.

If it makes you feel any better, you're not alone. The good news is if you figure out a way to conquer your day, you will be way ahead of everyone else. Here's a simple way:

Priority Rule One: Don't prioritize what's on your schedule... Schedule your priorities.

A true priority must exist somewhere other than your mind; it must find a place in your calendar. Since most people manage their work activities with their office calendar (such as Microsoft Outlook, Lotus Notes or Google Calendar), you must put your real priorities on your calendar. Your calendar represents your time, and if you don't take some of it for yourself so that you can work on your planned activity for the day, then you can be sure others will take it from you by scheduling meetings, phone calls, and conferences every moment of your day. Therefore, if you want to ensure you have the time to implement your own plan, then schedule it on your calendar. Block out your time for your own priorities before others do.

When you plan that one task you want to accomplish for the day, it's a good idea to schedule it on your calendar the night before. Now, when you walk into your office in the morning, not only will you know exactly what you want to accomplish, but you will have already reserved time to accomplish it. And the modern calendar is a wonderful thing. If you schedule to work on your task from 9:00 – 10:00a.m., and your calendar reminder pops up at 8:45 a.m., and then again at 8:55 a.m. with another reminder—there is a much greater chance that you will stop what you're doing to focus on this important scheduled activity. And if you schedule to work on that other task from 11:30 – 12:00 noon, you will likely get that complete as well. The rest of the time will probably be taken up by all those other things that go on during the day – but this time, not at the expense of your own priorities.

Priority Rule Two: Reserve your prime time for you.

Let's face it. The law of diminishing returns works against you every single day. We have all experienced the distractions, interruptions, emergencies and unscheduled events that conspire against us every day. I say fight back. Schedule your top priorities during your prime time. What is your prime time? It's the time that, barring all interruptions, you are at your most alert, your mind is at its sharpest, your focus is the clearest and your ability to get results and make decisions is the most effective. This is your prime time. When is yours?

Some people are most alert and work best first thing in the morning. Others take time to sharpen their mind and are better at developing concepts and making decisions later in the day. When is your mind the sharpest? Once you identify that time, you should use it to work on your most important or difficult tasks.

Now here's some interesting data. Most people tell me their prime time is in the morning, around 8:00 to 10:00 a.m. When asked how their typical day starts, however, they recount arriving at work at about 8:00 or 8:30 a.m., getting a cup of coffee, chatting with co-workers, checking paperwork on their desk, reviewing their e-mail, checking their calendar and then, only then, starting their day. At this point, the time is usually 9:30 or 10:00 a.m. They have just wasted their prime time, the time when their mind was at its best, on meaningless activities.

But even worse, some professionals have confided that although their prime time is morning, they actually get their most important work done after 5:00 p.m., when the office quiets down. Shocking, but not surprising. They are working on their most important activities when they are exhausted because they spent their prime time working on trivial tasks or other people's priorities. Remember, *you* control your day. Use your prime time for those activities that are important to you. A sharp mind gets the best results.

Priority Rule Three: Stay focused on the priority.

So let's say you actually scheduled your work for the day. You plan to work on next year's budget at 9:00 a.m. Just as you are about to begin working on this important project, your boss comes into your office and hands you a different assignment to work on. If you're like most people, you will immediately put down what you were about to do and instantly focus on the project your boss just handed you. Most people would do this without even asking a simple question: "When do you need it by?" or saying: "I was about to work on the budget, can I work on your request after lunch?"

Even worse—people react the exact same way when it's not even the boss interrupting them but a co-worker or someone from another department. Somehow we allow everyone else's priorities to take precedence over our own.

If you simply asked, "When does this need to be completed?" you would find that 99 percent of the time the answer is *not* immediately. In fact, your boss will probably be happy you are working on a key initiative, one that is a priority for him as well. In this case, you can continue to focus on your own priority until you have time to devote to this new project.

However, there is that rare instance when the request is actually urgent, such as an angry customer, production-line failure, network problems, you know, the things that come up at the worst possible time. In those instances, you should naturally stop what you're doing and help solve the problem;

but not before you re-schedule your important task to another time on your calendar. Commit to getting it done and follow through on your commitment.

This is how you plan your work and work your plan. Plan it and you will reap the rewards of Peak Performance.

Peak Performance Principles

► Spend five minutes the night before planning and scheduling what you want to accomplish tomorrow.

► Work on those initiatives that most closely align with core business objectives.

► Make your prime time your own time.

"It's not enough to just show up. You have to have a business plan."

CHAPTER 6
BRING ORDER TO CHAOS

YOU CAN MAKE IT IF YOU TRY

SLY AND THE FAMILY STONE, 1969

You can make it if you try
You can make it if you try
Push a little harder
Think a little deeper
Don't let the plastic bring you down

100 organized men can always defeat 1,000 disorganize ones.

—Nikolai Lenin

MAKE A LIST... CHECK IT TWICE!

Even Santa knew that the only way to keep track of endless things was to use a list. And this is based on hundreds of years of experience. Now we know that good organization is the hallmark of effective people. Organize your time, your day, your life, and you can accomplish more important things than the average professional. And it all starts with that simple, unassuming item that everyone cannot (and should not) live without—a good To-Do List.

The Almighty List

The list is the most powerful tool ever created by man for maximum productivity. Who knows who wrote the first one and it doesn't really matter; chiseled in some rock most probably. Every productive professional works from a list. On the other hand, those who consistently operate in crisis mode, reacting to events around them, feeling overwhelmed with tasks and responsibilities... are probably not using a list. Although they might appear busy, they are usually the most unproductive on the team.

If you ever feel overwhelmed with too much on your plate, if you have constantly conflicting demands and never enough time to get any one thing done, then making a list of every single thing you have to do will allow you to bring order to the chaos. The simple act of writing it all down will help you regain control and will also help you develop a strategy for results.

Without a list, how do you decide what to do? Actually, many people simply react to the person asking for something right now, or respond to some other incoming phone call or e-mail request. Without a list, you are most likely once again working on someone else's priorities, not your own.

If you start using a list today, you will immediately increase your efficiency by 25 percent. Guaranteed. (That's what Brian Tracy, the productivity guru, says.)

Create Action

The list puts your day into motion. It helps keep you on track, and there's nothing more satisfying than crossing things off as you go and seeing a list full of black lines at the end of the day.

So, to generate action and create that feeling of accomplishment, here's what to do:

Commit to using a list, really using it. Every time a new task, project or request reaches you; and if it will take you more than two minutes to resolve, resist the urge to act upon it immediately. Instead, add it to your list. An immediate request may appear to be urgent until you add it to your list and compare it to the other items. Then you may quickly realize that there a few other things already on your list that are actually more important to get done first. To stay organized, refuse to do anything until you have first added it to your list.

Add Clarity and Definition

Sometimes our own lists appear to work against us. Instead of creating a To Do List of action items, we have created a project list of concepts. The result is a list that is difficult to get done. Each item requires too much thought, planning or analysis to complete.

In training and coaching thousands of professionals, I have found that lack of time is not the major issue—although most think it is. The real problem is lack of clarity and definition about how to move forward with a specific item. Many

To Do Lists are a compilation of large projects rather than individual tasks.

Resolve to make your list work for you. Let it help you move forward on big projects and accomplish important tasks every day. You can do this by turning your To Do List into an *Action List*.

To make that happen, *begin every item on your list with an action word*. When you do that, you are describing the exact next step that is required to move this task, activity or project forward. Start every entry with a verb such as: review, e-mail, schedule, discuss, call, create, identify, meet, write, etc.

For example, let's say you're required to create a Division Budget. Most people would just put "division budget" on their list and be done with it. But that's where most people get bogged down. When they see "division budget" on their list, they're put off. They immediately perceive that this task will require so much time and effort to complete, that they defer it for later, otherwise known as "procrastinate." That's because it's a big project, not an individual task. To make it more doable, simply write down the specific next steps or actions that you need to take to create that division budget. Those specific steps become your Action List.

For your own clarification, it's still okay to write "Create Division Budget" at the top of your list. But now you need to do some thinking. Ask yourself, 'What are the next steps that need to get done in order to move this project along?' Perhaps you need to review and roll up the budgets created by your team. In order to do this, however, you must have their most recent budget. So, the first step under the main heading "Create Division Budget" would be: *Send e-mail to Dept. Managers requesting Q4 budgets*. Begin listing all of the other tasks that must be done in order to complete the budget underneath that.

Time Yourself

There's one more little addition to your Action List that most don't do but my clients find extremely helpful. It is actually key to helping you move these items along and easy to do. Next to each action, write down approximately how long it might take you to complete that task. For the example above, your action list item might say: Send e-mail to Dept Managers requesting 4Q budget numbers (5 min.). If all your actions also indicated a time element, you can quickly scan your list and easily determine what actions you can make progress on when you have ten to fifteen minutes available between meetings or thirty minutes before your next appointment.

List Example:
Typical List   Action List

Budget ► E-mail managers for 4Q budget numbers (5 min)
► Call Tom to discuss last year's budget (10 min)

Employee ► E-mail team to get started on self-appraisals (5 min)
Reviews ► List accomplishments for each team member (1 hr)

Ace Controls ► Develop format for Ace Controls Proposal (30 min)
Proposal ► Create list of product specs needed (30 min)

The upshot to putting all the action items on your list and then assigning times is that it keeps the rocks and pebbles at the forefront of your day and cuts down on the water and sand that could consume your precious time. And here's a bonus. If you look at the action list, there's a lot of time that's unaccounted for. You will actually find time to take care of the important water-type items — like catching up on e-mail, attending meetings and even planning your daughter's birthday party.

GIVE YOUR BOSS A DOSE OF REALITY

Once you have your action items listed out, then you need to prioritize. I can't stress this enough. Prioritize your list. Organize action items based on results. The natural tendency is to want to do the easiest things first. Please don't! Prioritizing your list helps point you in a productive direction.

Your priorities are those things that really matter – those activities that can most support your department goals, your boss's needs or your company's success. These are your goals, what you were hired to achieve and things that will make the greatest impact. Usually these are not the simple things, or the fun tasks, but rather the more time-consuming, attention-getting activities that can demonstrate your capabilities and initiative. Top of the list should include results-oriented activities that clearly support the company's core fundamentals or revenue goals. This is your opportunity to excel.

Once you have a prioritized Action List, it's a good idea to review it with your boss. You should do this on a regular basis for three good reasons:

Reason 1: Manage Up

I guarantee your boss has no idea the extent of the projects, tasks, and activities on your To Do List. Your manager is busy with his or her own responsibilities, and this is an opportunity to let them know what you have going on. Your manager hired you to take on work that he or she is responsible to perform. You are their surrogate to get much of that work completed as effectively as if they were doing it themselves. If the roles were reversed, I would bet you'd want to know as much as possible about what is going on in your personal domain. So do a great job of "managing up" and remove any of the mystery as to why you're there and what you are accomplishing. In the end it will help you to shine.

Reason 2: Get Agreement

Use this occasion to discuss priorities with your manager. Be sure you are in agreement on how you have prioritized your list. No matter how hard you work, if you are not focused on accomplishing tasks that your boss feels are the priorities, you will not be perceived as doing the right job or, for that matter, a good job. Your boss' priorities are your priorities.

Reason 3: Bring Clarity

Next time your boss gives you a project or task, you can refer to the list of priorities you both discussed and get confirmation on where this new project fits. Ask your boss: Is it more important than the current top three? Should you add it to the top or bottom of the list? You will notice that this type of interaction will cut down on "conflicting" priorities. Your priorities will become crystal clear.

TWO TICKETS TO PARADISE

If your boss walked into your office on a Monday morning holding two airline tickets to the Bahamas in his hand and said: "I won a pair of two first-class tickets over the weekend, but unfortunately I just can't go. I am willing to give you these tickets to a beautiful five star resort in the Bahamas. In order to receive these you need to accomplish your most important activities for the entire week by the end of today. If you do, you can have the tickets and start your vacation tomorrow." What would you do? Everyone I approached with this scenario has said: "I'm going to work my butt off to get those things done today!"

Here's where the infamous Pareto Principle kicks into action. The Pareto Principle is also known as the even more famous "80/20 Rule". It applies to most things in life: 80 percent of your best ideas come from 20 percent of your employees; 80 percent of your revenue comes from 20 percent of your customers; 80 percent of the time you wear the same 20 percent of your clothes; and, in this case, *80 percent of your results come from 20 percent of your time.* And now, with a luxury vacation to the Bahamas on the line, you only have 20 percent of your time to accomplish all the important things for the week!

The Pareto Principle is not a universal law, but rather a common effect. You can improve that ratio big time. The tasks you choose to work on are your priorities and should be your priorities every day of the week. These are the items at the top of your Action List. Imagine if you were able to modify this principle and increase your effectiveness even to 25 percent, or 35 percent, or even 50? What would your work life be like then? We're starting to envision the realm of rock stardom!

So Much To Do... So Little Time

If you're really good, you'll be rewarded with more responsibility and then your Action List is going to naturally become very long and may start to feel unwieldy. That list could easily contain 20, 30, 40 items or more. What happens when you look at that enormous list? I have been told — it's demoralizing. It's overwhelming. I feel anger and frustration. I feel defeated and deflated before I even start.

In an effort to shorten the list, as well as enjoy the pleasure of crossing things off, people have a tendency to do the easiest things first. Yes, it's true. By accomplishing the many small and easy tasks, the list appears to be getting shorter. But are you accomplishing the priorities and goal related activities that yield results? Are you taking care of the rocks or simply adding water and building more sandcastles instead of working toward achieving your goals. Think - Two Tickets to Paradise!

The Path of Least Resistance

The natural tendency of human nature is to follow the path of least resistance. In terms of personal performance and time management, this means that we have a natural tendency to start on small tasks, thinking that as soon as we get warmed up we will launch into our big tasks and be more productive. But this is rarely the case.

In the famous Star Trek TV show entitled "The Trouble with Tribbles," a rogue space trader comes aboard the Starship Enterprise with hidden contraband. Turns out his prized booty are two very small, fluffy and adorable creatures the size of a hamster. The crew is so taken by the extremely soothing sensation from simply holding these little guys that, before anyone knows it, everyone has one as a pet. But, to everyone's surprise they breed faster than rabbits at warp speed. Before they can say "Beam me up Scotty," the ship is overrun with Tribbles in every air vent, compartment and on every deck.

Well, little tasks are like Tribbles. When you start on them they begin to multiply until you never run out. Remember sweet Suzanne in Chapter 1? She was so busy responding to everyone's requests she found no time to focus on what really mattered. She simply seemed to create more and more small tasks that "needed" to be completed. She became swamped with Tribbles. When you go down that path, you become exhausted by the end of the day from working relentlessly on so many little details, yet accomplish little of great value. Start with your most important work first.

▶

You will achieve greater results if you move three things a mile instead of 100 things an inch.

KNOW YOUR PRIORITIES

If you have a truly difficult time getting the important stuff done or are simply overwhelmed by the number of things listed on your list, then there's something else you can do. On the right side of your Action List, about two inches in from the right margin, draw a line down the paper. At the top, write "Daily Priorities." Now list four important things you can accomplish in about two hours and write them down. Be sure to also jot down the approximate time it will take to complete each task so that the total time does not exceed two hours. This "sub-list" will now become your Priority Action List for the day. If you expect to have more time available, create a longer list. Experience has shown that most professionals rarely have more than two hours per day available to focus without interruption. If your day will be very busy, create a list of only one or two items. Do not fill up your entire day with priority tasks. As you know, you will always need time to interact with your co-workers, respond to last-minute requests and finish unexpected projects.

Your shortened priority list will help you focus on the few things you want to get done. Because the list is right next to your Action List, you can see how the two are working together, or not, and plan accordingly.

There's another plus point to having a Daily Priorities List. When you look at a list of four items, you're not overwhelmed. You feel confident, a bit inspired and motivated to accomplish them. And you'll be extremely satisfied when you have crossed off all the items on your Priority List by the end of the day.

Like any good habit in life, it takes repetition. When you repeatedly concentrate on your top priorities, you will rapidly develop the habit of high performance. With this, you will soon be getting two to three times as much done every day as anyone else who works around you. And you will feel terrific about yourself as you move closer to stardom!

Peak Performance Principles

► *Create an Action List of everything you need to get done.*
► *Prioritize your list.*
► *Share it with your boss.*
► *Make your boss' priorities your priorities.*

CHAPTER 7
IT'S NOW OR NEVER

DAYDREAM
LOVIN' SPOONFUL, 1966

What a day for a daydream
What a day for a day dreamin' boy
And I'm lost in a daydream
Dreamin' 'bout my bundle of joy

And even if time ain't really on my side
It's one of those days for taking a walk outside
I'm blowing the day to take a walk in the sun
And fall on my face on somebody's new-mown lawn

*If you wait too long for the perfect moment, the perfect
moment will pass you by.*

—Confucius

MASTER PROCRASTINATOR

The Action List along with the Daily Priorities List is designed
to get you and then keep you in action all throughout the
day. But inevitably, despite all your best intentions, that damn
"P" word rears its ugly head and your day goes to hell.

"I'm not in the mood right now."
"I can't do this, it's too overwhelming."
"I'll do it after I check my e-mail and get a cup of coffee."

Sound familiar? Getting things done is easy when it's something we enjoy doing, but unfortunately, not all tasks are fun.
Even when something really needs to get done, most people
have become very good at finding just the right excuses for
putting it off:

"I'll work on that when I have more energy."
"I'll start that project first thing in the morning."
"It's not really due for another couple of days."
"I'll get to it right after lunch."
"I should get some input first."
"Let me just check the online news to see what's happened today."
"I just want to see if I have new Facebook messages."
"I have a few other things to take care of right now."
"My computer is too slow right now."
"Just one quick game of solitaire."
"Tom needs my help with something."
. . . And on and on. . .

Hmm, it would appear that when it comes to rocks and pebbles we love to contemplate our navels and procrastinate by adding an excessive amount of water and way too much sand.

We are all expert procrastinators. We have been procrastinating since before we knew the meaning of the word; since the first time our parents told us to pick up our toys and we decided there were plenty of other things we'd rather be doing. And since then, we have worked hard perfecting that skill in elementary school with book reports, in high school with exams, and in college with last-minute term papers and all-night cramming sessions. And now we are so very good at it, we often procrastinate while giving the appearance that we're hard at work doing our job. If only we could get paid for procrastinating, we'd all be filthy rich!

But alas, procrastination is the enemy. It robs us of time and makes us feel guilty about our lack of accomplishment. Procrastinators work as many hours in the day as other people, and often even more, but they invest their time in the wrong tasks. Procrastinators often become the complainers— the people who moan and groan about how they don't like their job, their boss, their cubicle. They complain because they have low morale. They have low morale because they don't produce anything that makes them proud. They struggle to show real meaningful results from their work.

Procrastinators sometimes hide behind doing things for others or responding to those whose demands are loudest. Perhaps they waste their time chatting, surfing the internet, playing solitaire online, or checking their social networking site. Whatever method they chose to avoid that dreaded task, there is little time left for the important tasks.

Another common cause of procrastination is feeling overwhelmed by the project. You might not know where to begin. Or you may doubt that you have the skills or resources you think you need to do a good job. So you seek comfort in doing tasks you know you're capable of completing. The very sad unfortunate truth is – those real priorities aren't going away; important things rarely do. In fact, they seem to keep building up. Yikes!

Daydreaming or Creating?

A programmer was sitting at his desk staring out the window and making absolutely no attempt to look busy. This drove his co-workers crazy. So they complained to the boss who asked them how long the programmer had been behaving this way. When they told him, the boss instructed them to get the programmer coffee, lunch, or anything else his heart desired and to make sure that he wasn't interrupted. When the co-workers complained again, the boss explained: "The last few times he acted like this, he came up with unique code that was worth millions of dollars. So whatever you do, don't disturb him. Let him create!"

Everyone works differently. The key is to be flexible enough to accept diversity, but realistic enough to identify avoidance and irresponsibility, both in ourselves and in others.

Procrastination Never Wins

Not only does procrastination never win, it causes us to feel defeated, deflated and disappointed in ourselves. Even worse, procrastination can cause great harm. Imagine if a paramedic stopped for coffee on the way to the scene of an accident – it could mean the difference between life and death. Or if you waited until the last minute to book the conference exhibit space and your company's new trade show booth got stuck in the back corner behind the restrooms. This could mean lost revenue, angry management and a career derailment. Nothing good comes from procrastination. Don't allow it to get the better of you.

THREE EASY STEPS TO DEFEAT PROCRASTINATION

Yes! It's possible! Here's the three step process that will help you defeat procrastination every time. All you have to do is apply it.

Step 1: Recognize that you are procrastinating.
Admit it. Even if it appears that you are working very hard, are you really working on those things that matter?
Here are some hints that you might be procrastinating:

► Filling your day with the easy things on your To Do List, just to cross them off.
► Reading the same e-mail more than once without making any progress on it.
► Sitting down to start your high-priority task but almost immediately getting up to get a cup of coffee or check your e-mail.
► Ignoring an item on your Action List day after day, even though you know it's important.
► Often saying "Yes" to unimportant tasks or requests.
► Taking care of personal business during your prime time.
► ...and, well you know you have so many of your own creative ways, don't you?

OK, then, if you are ready to admit you are procrastinating, you can move on to step 2.

Step 2: Figure out why you are procrastinating.
This can depend on both you and the task.

► Are you procrastinating because you hate this task? Would you prefer to be doing something more fun?

▶ Or, are you procrastinating because you find the task overwhelming? You don't know where or how to begin.

These are the two categories into which 99.9 percent of all procrastinating fall. In order to control it, you must understand why you're doing it.

Step 3: Get over it! And here's how.

If you're putting something off because you just don't want to do it and you can't delegate it to someone else, then you need to get some skin in the game, something in it for you. You need to reward yourself.

Rewards work very well whether you are being rewarded by someone else or even by yourself. Promise yourself something special if you get this project done by a particular time. For example, you might plan to go to your favorite restaurant for lunch if you finish the dreaded task by noon time. Or you can leave the office a few minutes early to catch your son's soccer game if you complete the task by 2:00 pm. Buy yourself the CD you've been wanting or bring home a movie to watch. Create a reward that will make it worth your while to finish this unpleasant task. It's a win-win. Not only do you complete that dreaded task, but you also get something you like out of the deal.

When I worked at a technology firm in Boston, I was responsible for a customer installation report due the last Friday of every month. I absolutely hated this cumbersome, time-consuming and really boring task. I learned early on, however, that rewards were a good motivator. I also had a favorite restaurant, the Sweet Onion, which was a little too far away for a quick work lunch. But I made a deal with myself. If I finished my report by 11:30 a.m., I would meet my friend for lunch at the Sweet Onion. Well, I did this and my perspective on the installation report was forever changed. I actually looked forward to the last Friday of every month as I would meet my close friend at my favorite restaurant. It was worth a couple of hours of tedium for a great meal and a fun lunch with a buddy!

However, if you're procrastinating because you find the task overwhelming, too complicated, difficult or big, then your strategy must be to break down the project into small, more manageable tasks—as small and simple as possible. For example, you might write down the questions you have about the project, or request a copy of a similar completed report, or identify the final format required. Then, do the simplest thing first. By working on the simplest component, you actually make a dent in the project and often start to build some momentum. You will also develop confidence in your ability to actually move forward on the dreaded task at hand. It is said that confidence precedes competence, so when you're confident that you can do something, you are able to do it, and often do it well.

A carrot is better than a stick

If you procrastinate, you are no different than everybody else. But if you defeat procrastination, you will set yourself apart from others. Remember that a carrot is better than a stick even though they may both accomplish the same thing. But which is more motivating? What will make you more likely to tackle the job at hand? Would you rather have the reward of action or the stress and consequences of inaction? If you like carrots and you associate the jobs at hand with getting a reward at the end; you are less likely to get in your own way.

Defeating procrastination is key to taking control of your day, your life and your success.

Peak Performance Principles
► Admit you are procrastinating.
► Figure out why you are procrastinating.
► Get over it!

"You've got pussyfooting from 10 to 11, shilly-shallying until 12, then hemming and hawing the rest of the afternoon."

CHAPTER 8
ONE OF THESE DAYS IS NONE OF THESE DAYS

FLY LIKE AN EAGLE
STEVE MILLER, 1976

Time keeps on slippin', slippin', slippin'
Into the future
Time keeps on slippin', slippin', slippin'
Into the future

I want to fly like an eagle
To the sea
Fly like an eagle
Let my spirit carry me
I want to fly like an eagle
Till I'm free
Oh, Lord, through the revolution

Without a deadline, baby, I wouldn't do nothin'.

—Duke Ellington

LEARN TO LOVE DEADLINES

What happens to you when you hear the word 'deadline'? If you're like most people, you cringe. You slink away to the water cooler, hoping that deadline doesn't apply to you.

I suspect this is likely because (a) people are so caught up in all the time-consuming tasks of their day or (b) they already have so much other stuff on their plate. Either way, putting a time limit on getting a project done downright scares the crap out people. How is it humanly possible to get it done by close of business Thursday?

Deadlines aren't the bad boys of your work day. In fact, deadlines are the magic that make things happen. But it's not as simple as that. To make it happen, a deadline has to be just right. Make it too short—you truly don't have enough time to do it, and you'll end up frustrated. Give yourself too much time and you'll lose interest—or get involved in other projects and forget or ignore that first deadline altogether.

Setting deadlines, however, will not do the trick if you don't prioritize first. The rock or pebble deadlines must always take precedent over water deadlines. Never lose sight of what moves you forward and what you are trying to accomplish.

Deadlines get results.

A successful deadline is one that causes you to stretch but not break. Make it a challenge and challenge yourself to meet it. No time to waste, no time to kick back, you only have time to focus on results. Meeting a challenging deadline provides a real sense of accomplishment and pride.

Seth Godin, bestselling author, writes in his blog:

"You don't realize how much you need a boss until you don't have one. But here's what we know about good bosses... Bosses create deadlines and stick to them.

A boss gives you the momentum you need to get through the stuff that takes perseverance. The main thing that ends the career of a free-agent is the lack of a hand pushing on the back, someone handing out assignments and waiting for the deliverables. Who keeps you going when you don't feel like doing it?

If you don't have a boss, you may need to invent one."

Make It Public

Want to make doubly sure you get it done? *Make a public commitment.* Announce your intention to get the project done by a specific date and time. Tell your co-worker you'll have the report to them by 5:00 p.m. today or tell your manger you'll have the first draft of the customer presentation completed by Friday. You will. You said it aloud and committed to completing the task. You have set expectations and you don't want to disappoint.

Just Do It. Something.

Okay. Are you *really* ready to make it happen? Want to make triple-sure? Then *do something right now* towards meeting that deadline. Sometimes the hardest part of any job is simply starting it. So do something, anything, right now. Even if it means merely gathering all the documents you need to put together that final report and putting them in a neat pile on your desk or getting that opening title slide done for your PowerPoint presentation. You have now started the process. You signaled to your mind that you are serious and ready to meet the challenge.

This book is the perfect example of just that. I had the great desire to write this book but found it very tough to start. It appeared to be such a big and difficult project. Who has the time to write a book? Well, apparently a lot of people do as is evidenced when you walk into a Barnes & Noble or log on to Amazon.com. So why can't I get it done? After teaching this deadline principle to a thousand professionals I finally decided to apply it to myself.

Once I broke down my book project into manageable components, I set aggressive, but realistic deadlines for getting each piece done. Then I was brave and did the unthinkable. I sent out an e-mail to over fifty close friends and family members. I announced that I was embarking on a book and hoped to share it with them by the end of the year. Yikes! Believe me, my hand shook as I pressed that SEND key, but I haven't looked back since. I did not want to disappoint!

The miracle of accomplishment sits ready to emerge. Set a deadline that causes you to stretch but not break. Announce your intention. Do something right now to get you started. And you will get it done!

Peak Performance Principles
► Create a deadline that causes you to stretch, but not break.
► Make a public commitment to getting it done.
► Do something right now to get started.

CHAPTER 9
COPING IN A SANDSTORM OF INTERRUPTIONS

YOU TALK TOO MUCH
JOE JONES, 1961

You talk too much
You worry me to death
You talk too much
You worry my pet
You just talk
Talk too much

*The average American worker has fifty interruptions a day,
of which seventy percent have nothing to do with work.*

—W. Edwards Deming

PLEASE JUST STOP TALKING!

Interruptions. Interruptions. Interruptions. They come from all sides: your boss, your co-workers, clients, vendors, friends and sometimes, even strangers. We have developed a culture that encourages interruptions. "Gotta minute?" This actually translates to: 'Let's talk about my issue right now for the next fifteen minutes.' And usually, the response is, "Sure!"

Up to this point, I've been giving you some tips and hints on how to plan your day so that you can be more productive. Now, in the next three chapters, I need to address the most common time-suckers we face every day: people wanting to talk, e-mails demanding attention, and meetings that get no traction — the sand and the water, although it seems more like quicksand.

If you're serious about mastering your day, focusing on important things and achieving peak performance, then you have to first make a determined effort to manage the inevitable interruptions. But let's face it, when your co-worker, who is also your friend, stops by your office and begins to excitedly tell you about their weekend in New York—down to every detail—you feel like you're in a quandary. They are sharing not only information, but camaraderie. So how do you tell your friend and co-worker you're really too busy without bursting their bubble or hurting their feelings?

Of course excited co-workers and friends aren't the only problem. When you are asked to be on the Christmas Party Committee or help with a random project by a longtime colleague, how do you turn them down and say, "No, thank you," without sacrificing your relationships?

The answer is: with honesty and common consideration of the other person.

Shhhh...

So let's deal with the talker, or long storyteller. Here is how you send someone away when they just walk into your office and start chatting non-stop about an issue that is obviously important to them, but not to you. You might even be genuinely interested, but simply don't have the time. You would love to talk, but this is the kind of sand that you have to earn. You haven't completed even one of your priority tasks. You're committed to working everyday to achieve peak performance, and so you're in a dilemma. You need to very nicely, but firmly, get your friend to just stop talking!

The most important element of any personal communication is empathy. So start on a personal note. Focus on the person directly, make eye contact, and say their name. Yes, validate and recognize them by saying their name, interrupting their conversation.

Saying their name not only acknowledges them, but it magically makes the person stop talking — often in mid-sentence. Once they have been acknowledged, they will actually pause and give you the floor. This is your moment to respond.

Seize this moment! Immediately say something positive or responsive to the person. You might say, "Nancy, you always have such great weekend experiences," or, "Bob, sounds like you are really frustrated by what's going on in your department." No matter what they're talking about, it's usually possible to find something positive or responsive to say. And because we want to build relationships, not destroy them, we say it even if we aren't in the mood. What you just did was demonstrate that you sincerely care about what the other person has to share with you.

Now is your opportunity to send them away, yet still feeling good about their interaction with you. Add to your response why you can't talk now but perhaps you can catch up with them later. For example: "Nancy, you always have such great weekend experiences. I'd love to hear about it, but I'm working on an important project right now; how about if I stop by your desk around lunchtime?"

You have validated the other person, let them know you are interested and suggested a better time. Similarly, you might say to Bob: "Bob, sounds like you are really frustrated with what's going on in your department; but I have to finish this report by this afternoon. How about if I swing by your office at the end of the day to hear all the details?"

This three-step process will work almost all of the time. On occasion, you may have to repeat the person's name. They may be so busy talking; they actually did not hear you acknowledge them. Repeating their name usually does the trick.

▶───────────────────────────────

Get them to stop talking –
1. Acknowledge the person by saying their name.
2. Say something positive or responsive about their situation.
3. Let them know why now is not a good time and suggest another time to catch up.

───────────────────────────────

The Magic Bullet
Say your friend still wants to stick around, or you are so engrossed in your work that you don't want to exert the mental energy to engage in the conversation, ever. There's one simple statement that is the magic bullet. It will scare off most anyone. Ready? It's "I'm working on a deadline." If they come back with, "What deadline?" - tell them what it is or simply respond "my deadline." Most people want to stay

away from deadlines, yours or theirs. And here's the best part. You're not being dishonest!

The beauty of the pickle jar system of life management is you have now created deadlines for yourself that you are committed to meeting. As I've mentioned, most people are intimidated by deadlines. It's a great conversation killer because they worry you might ask them to help you meet yours. The typical thought is: "Let me get out of your way, then," and as far away from that deadline as possible.

JUST SAY NO

Sometimes, these types of interruptions are tough because not only is the person approaching you someone you like and respect, but they are making a sincere request. Just remember, time is your most valuable asset, and this is all about learning to manage it with some smarts. Learning to say "No" is an act of self-preservation. Those people, who don't master the ability to say no are often overloaded with random work and responsibilities that shouldn't be theirs. They become less efficient and increasingly stressed and ultimately helpful to no one, including themselves.

The need-to-say-no situation is a bit different than the random person stopping by for a chat. We are talking about a direct request for participation or assistance, but a request you just don't want or have the time to fulfill. So when you just need to say, "No," know you can say it without alienating the other person. Do it by using the classic **USA Method:**

U – **Understand what they are asking you is important to them.**
Never say no without demonstrating that you fully understand the importance of the request. If the requestor

doesn't feel you understand why this is important, they will likely continue to explain the value or significance of their appeal.

S – State your situation.
Explain exactly why you must refuse their request.

A – Action or another solution.
If possible, try to propose another option or alternative to help them resolve their situation.

The USA Method allows you to demonstrate empathy with an *understanding* statement, then explain the *situation*, and provide an *alternative*.

You will be both effective and polite saying no without causing offense, possibly helping in another way. When you say no using the USA method, you will be saying no in a very diplomatic and empathetic way, causing no resentment, hurt feelings or sending the wrong message.

For example: Bob asks, "Steve, can you call the twelve Regional Reps and find out if they will be attending the sales meeting next week? I haven't heard from all of them, and I'm trying to finalize the numbers."

Steve is thinking to himself: 'I don't have time to call the Regional Reps. I have several things on my plate that are much more important for me to get done today. But how can I say no without offending Bob?'

Apply the USA Method: "Bob, I know how important the sales meeting is and the need to get a handle on head-count..." (U), "But I am working on a project that needs to be completed by this afternoon" (S). "Perhaps someone else on the team can make some phone calls on your behalf." (A)

This method works for personal requests as well: Tom

asks, "Susan, will you join the Community Board this year? We really need someone with accounting experience."

Use the USA Method to decline: "Tom, I know the Community Board is really important for maintaining our neighborhood, but I have been traveling quite a bit for business and can't devote the time. Perhaps you can call me when you have specific accounting questions and I can respond if I have the expertise."

The reason the USA Method is so effective is because of the "U." Once you let the requestor know you understand that their request is important to them, then they can accept and feel good about your decision. If you simply respond: "I'm sorry, but I'm too busy to help you right now," then the other person will try to explain why their request is important and convince you to comply. Be diplomatic. It takes the sting out of "no."

Relationships are Important

Although sometimes you'd like to be left alone, most of the time you are happy to have your co-workers around, to share successes, frustrations, celebrations, and challenges. So remember your goal is to build and maintain relationships. When you ask someone to "leave you alone" or tell them, "No, I can't help you out," be sure to do it in a way that continues to assure them that you care. Apply these methodologies to all your relationships and you will maintain control of your time without sacrificing friendship.

Peak Performance Principles
► Say their name and they will stop talking!
► Let them know you understand what they are asking you to do is important, even if you can't help.
► Be diplomatic; but remember — your priorities must come first.

"And who shall I say wants to see him, and interupt his efforts to finish work early and get on the golf course."

CHAPTER 10
USING THE POWER OF OTHERS

I CAN HELP
BILLY SWAN, 1975

If you got a problem, don't care what it is
If you need a hand, I can assure you this
I can help, I got two strong arms
I can help
It would sure do me good, to do you good
Let me help

The best executive is the one who has sense enough to pick good men to do what he wants done, and self-restraint enough to keep from meddling with them while they do it.

—Theodore Roosevelt

THE ART OF DELEGATING

Delegating is good. It can be a great tool for helping motivate, train and build self-confidence in the people who work around you. Taking on new responsibilities can really help them to realize their full potential. But for everyone who is reading this, know that it is also a very productive means to ensure that you are freed to focus on what matters most to you, the more strategic issues — to really concentrate on the rocks in your jar.

Many professionals are afraid to delegate. They typically want to retain control. Tasks should be done their way and slight variations on their particular approach tend to be hard to deal with. They aim for perfection, only to ultimately slow down their own personal progress. We all have this tendency to get in our own way over a matter of personal pride. Whether you are an executive, manager, team leader or independent contributor, knowing how to delegate well can make an enormous difference to your personal forward momentum and success, as well as the success and effectiveness of your team.

Delegating is important in every business environment. When you delegate, you empower the other person. You say: I believe in you. I trust you. If done well, delegating can inspire commitment and develop a more satisfied, productive and effective employee.

Captain Kirk knew how to delegate

Captain James Kirk, commander of the Starship Enterprise, was not the brainiest guy on the ship. And he knew it. He depended on Mr. Spock, his first officer, with his highly logical intellect, Dr. McCoy, with all the medical knowledge available to mankind in the twenty third century, and Scotty, the chief engineer, who had the technical know-how to keep the ship running even when it was under attack by Andorians or Klingons. So what was Kirk's skill set? He had leadership. He was the essence of the dynamic manager, a guy who had the passion to inspire and he knew how to delegate. In every episode, his life depended on it.

DELEGATE THE RESULT, NOT THE PROCESS

Delegate the result; the process is none of your business. This usually works. When you ask your spouse to cook dinner, expect a delicious meal and stay out of the kitchen. When you ask your gardener to maintain your lawn, don't knit-pick on which direction the grass gets cut. Simply be happy with a neat, trimmed, lush and healthy lawn. And when you ask a co-worker to do a project, be sure to let them know the results you expect, but let them decide how to complete or implement the process. Unless they ask for help, empower the worker to successfully achieve the task on their own, but be certain that they completely understand the end result you are looking for.

You will find that when you give a true professional the opportunity to be creative, use their resources, take the initiative and develop a strategy and approach, the results you get will exceed your expectations.

Duke Basketball Coach Mike Krzyzewski (Coach K) expressed this concept best in his book, *Leading With Heart*. "If you put a plant in a jar, it will take the shape of the jar. But if you allow the plant to grow freely, twenty jars might not be able to hold it. The freedom to grow personally, the freedom to make mistakes and learn from them, the freedom to work hard, and the freedom to be yourself — these four freedoms should be guaranteed by every leader in every organization."

Certainly, it is important to agree upon the criteria and standards by which the outcome will be judged, but then get out of the way. The empowered employee will enthusiastically approach their task, proudly figure out the process and hopefully give you the results you expect. If all goes according to plan, you now have one less thing on your plate and one more effective member of your team producing real results.

▶

The Janitor

If you tell the janitor to empty the baskets on Tuesdays and Fridays, the baskets will be emptied on Tuesdays and Fridays. If the baskets overflow on Wednesday, they will be emptied on Friday as specified. If instead you said to empty the baskets as often as necessary, the janitor would decide how often and adapt to special circumstances. By leaving the decision up to the janitor you will apply his/her specific knowledge to the challenge. Consider this frankly: do you want to be an expert on emptying waste baskets? If not, delegate it to someone who gets paid to do it well.

Know What You Want

Ambiguity kills any hope of getting the outcome you want. When you delegate, communicate the result you want, and then help that person accomplish the task by giving specific and relevant information about what, why, when, who, where and how you want it done. Too often people have not decided exactly what they *actually* want before making a request of someone else. This is something we've all experienced in our everyday lives, even over trivial matters. Imagine this typical conversation:

Carly —Let's go out to dinner!
Jeremy—OK. How about Chinese?
Carly—No, I'm not in the mood for Chinese.
Jeremy—How about Mexican?
Carly—Na, I just had Mexican yesterday.
Jeremy—OK, how about Italian?
Carly—No, that's too heavy.
Jeremy—Want a burger?
Carly— Not really in the mood for a burger.
Jeremy—What do you want?
Carly—I don't know?
Jeremy – OK, when you figure out what you want, let me know.

If you don't know what you want, will anything really satisfy you? To delegate effectively, you must know right upfront what you *really* want, not just what you *don't* want! Clarity is the absolute key to getting your desired results.

Set-up for Success

To enable someone else to do a good job for you, you must ensure that:

A. They know what you want.
B. They have the authority to achieve it.
C. They know how to do it.
D. They have the required information and resources to get it done.

Put it in writing. If possible, put it in writing so there is no misunderstanding. Ask for feedback and questions. If possible, demonstrate or show an example of the expected results.

Give total authority to complete the job. Let everyone know that this individual is now in charge and has been empowered to make final decisions regarding this project. Don't allow others to come to you with their suggestions or disagreements. Refer them back to the person who has been delegated the task and make sure you give that person the authority to make all the decisions required to achieve the results.

For example, if Sara is delegated to manage the logistics for the Sales Conference in Puerto Rico, then be sure the team understands and accepts that Sara has final decision-making authority on such details as room allocation, entertainment selection, menu options and activities. Sara is encouraged to ask for input, but the team must be directed to coordinate their activities through her and respect the decisions she makes. In this case, you will find that Sara will take her job more seriously, evaluate options more thoroughly and work even harder because she knows she has been entrusted with this important responsibility.

Ensure they have the ability to do an excellent job. The key is to delegate gradually. If you present someone with a task which is daunting, one for which they don't have enough experience or knowledge to complete, then odds are they won't meet expectations and will ultimately come away from the experience de-motivated. However, if you give them a small task and continue to build on it with more responsibility and greater results, you will be training a professional with the skills and motivation you can count on. It's the difference between asking people to scale a sheer wall and providing them with a staircase.

If a project requires additional resources, be sure to help provide access to whatever is needed to get the job done well and on time. Help by providing access to company information, cooperation from another team member or department, direction or information from others on the management team. Knowing that the necessary knowledge and resources are available will give your team member the confidence to undertake their new responsibility.

Questions lead to more questions. Don't hover over your employee but maintain open lines of communication so they feel comfortable turning to you for help. But most importantly, avoid making decisions which the employee is capable of making on their own.

Duke basketball's Coach K likes to ask questions, lots of questions. He explains: "If a player is looking for an answer, for instance, rather than just telling him straight out, I may ask him a series of questions so that he'll think for himself and try to reason the answer out. That way, he'll remember the solution better and be more likely to implement it."

Help them build confidence and you will be rewarded with an employee and team member you can trust to work hard and make the right decisions on your behalf.

Unfortunately, the power to delegate doesn't come with an instruction book of success. Successful delegating is not always intuitive and many can benefit from some basic guidelines to help ensure the results you want:

There are many good reasons to delegate:
► Allows managers to spend time on their most valuable tasks.
► Divides responsibilities or work effort to create a more efficient process.
► Increases employee commitment to the organization.

▶ Shows confidence in the individual and positively develops your team.

Some things lend themselves to delegating more than others:
▶ Low priority tasks (high priority for someone else).
▶ Projects that require technical or unique expertise.
▶ Jobs and tasks that someone has more experience performing.
▶ Tasks that someone else would enjoy more than you.
▶ Cross-training so that work can continue without interruption.
▶ Projects or activities that will enable a person to grow professionally.
▶ Projects or task that can expose an employee to another segment of the business or a different professional team.

Don't even think about delegating when it comes to:
▶ Motivating your team.
▶ Evaluating performance or success.
▶ Rewarding employees.
▶ Dealing with personal challenges.
▶ Attending an employee's family event.
▶ Managing crises.
▶ Creating policy.

"Scott, when you see Debbie, tell her I said she did a good job."
Don't ever delegate managing or motivating your team!

Peak Performance Principles
▶ Delegate the result, not the process.
▶ Delegate to empower; provide total authority.
▶ Ensure all the resources are available for success.

"I start my day by making a list of everything
I need to do . . . and who I can get
to do it for me."

CHAPTER 11
ARE YOU STONED OR JUST CHECKING E-MAIL?

MESSAGE IN BOTTLE
POLICE, 1979

Walked out this morning
Don't believe what I saw
A hundred billion bottles
Washed up on the shore
Seems I'm not alone at being alone
A hundred billion castaways
Looking for a home

I'll send an SOS to the world
I hope that someone gets my
Message in a bottle

If e-mail had been around when the telephone was invented, people would have said 'Hey forget e-mail. With this new telephone invention I can actually talk to people.'

—Anonymous

AIR, WATER AND E-MAIL

E-mail. We love it; we hate it. It is now a mainstay in our lives. After all, when was the last time you sent a paper letter by the postal service? You could no more live without e-mail than you could live without your cell phone.

E-mail, interestingly, can be pebbles, sand, or water. Some e-mails are incredibly important and critical to accomplishing your goals; others couldn't be further from this. But we can all agree that e-mail has become an overwhelming distraction, one of the biggest time-sucks of our day. E-mail, the killer app that is at the core of the computer revolution, has both made our lives easier, better, more fun, interesting, entertaining and even productive. . . and a tremendous waste of time. So, let's make use of the good and minimize the bad. Let's take control of this runaway train.

Most professionals say that they receive over one hundred real e-mails every day. According to the "experts," it takes the average person about two minutes to deal with each e-mail. If that's accurate, then it takes the average employee over two hours to read and respond to e-mail daily. And this doesn't take into account those messages that take five, ten or twenty-minutes to deal with.

Yet, ask anyone if they are willing to give up e-mail and they can't bear the thought. E-mail has become our lifeline to the rest of our individual worlds. So, use it well and reap the benefits; otherwise, we're all destined to become its slave.

How did we come to this?

In the old world of typing, printing, and stamping, the sender thought twice about going through the effort to send a copy of their letter to others. That meant more typing, printing and stamping. Was that extra copy really worth the added effort and expense? Careful thought was given to every cc:'ed carbon copy on the letter. But not anymore. The world has changed.

Now you can quickly and easily send an e-mail for free to any number of people with just a few keystrokes. So it seems we've collectively decided to include everyone on everything. And everyone is returning the favor. Jokes, thoughts, personal responses, ramblings, and now Facebook, Twitter, DIGG — you name it, are all integrated in the same e-mail batch with those important few that contain critical information or other important correspondences.

Surveys indicate that more than 40 percent of respondents check their e-mail immediately as a new message arrives. Given that it takes an average person approximately twelve minutes to re-engage in a task once his or her concentration has been broken, it's no wonder that a majority of respondents feel that their volume of e-mail prevents them from completing other job-related activities.

ARE YOU STONED, OR JUST CHECKING E-MAIL?

Believe it or not, e-mail might do more damage to your brain than smoking pot, according to a study commissioned by Hewlett Packard (Great Britain) and carried out by the Institute of Psychiatry at Kings College, London.

The study of 1,000 adults found their intelligence declined as tasks were interrupted by incoming e-mails and texts. The average reduction of ten IQ points is more than double the four point loss associated with smoking marijuana. In fact, a ten point drop is also associated with missing a full night of sleep, the report said.

The study warned of a rise in "infomania," a term coined by Hewlett Packard, to describe the consequence of people becoming addicted to e-mail and text messages. "This is a very real and widespread phenomenon," said Dr. Glenn Wilson, author of the research. "Infomania, if unchecked, will damage a worker's performance by reducing their mental sharpness."

According to Discover magazine that published the results, researchers asked two sets of subjects to take IQ tests. One group was encouraged to check e-mail and respond to instant messages while taking the test. The second group took the test with no distractions.

Not surprisingly, the distracted group didn't fare as well, performing an average of 10 points lower than the control group. The same study was then performed on a group "intoxicated by marijuana" that showed less than half the point loss. With these results, researchers concluded that "multitasking is worse for your ability to concentrate than getting stoned."

Here are some more interesting observations that came from the study —

► 62 percent of workers are addicted to checking messages even when out of the office and on vacation.
► Most adults will respond to an e-mail immediately or within ten minutes.
► One in five is "happy" to interrupt a business or social meeting to respond to an e-mail or text message.
► Yet 89 percent of those surveyed found it rude for colleagues to do so.

Making matters even worse, almost a third of respondents said that *fewer* than 1 in 4 office e-mail messages left them with a positive impression and motivated them to want to work harder with that person.

It's no wonder we are frustrated by e-mail. Based on many of the e-mails we receive and work habits we witness, we're left wondering, "Are you stoned, or just checking e-mail?"

THE 14 HOLY COMMANDMENTS OF E-MAIL

The time has come to bring some order to this chaos. There's no question that e-mail can be an incredibly valuable tool when used effectively. You simply have to learn to control this dominating beast. So let's move out of the Stone Age and onto a new age. It's an age ruled by the 14 Holy Commandments of E-mail. And thou shall respect the power of e-mail.

1. Summarize the e-mail in the Subject line.

People scan their IN box by subject. Make the subject meaningful enough so that readers can quickly decide if this e-mail is relevant to them. You need to help your e-mail recipient know if this is a rock, pebble, sand, or water e-mail so they can respond accordingly. Help the reader by summarizing the contents in the subject. Cut to the chase with the critical information. The reader should be able to jump right into the e-mail prepared for the discussion and not have to sift through all the content to get to the main points.

BAD E-MAIL	GOOD E-MAIL
RE: Product Update	RE: Gismo scan features on hold until Q4

2. When forwarding or replying, summarize the issues and key discussion points.

When forwarding or replying to a conversation string, start off your message with a brief summary to give the reader a perspective on the key issues being discussed. Don't expect the reader to understand your reply based on the attached string of six or seven messages. Not only is this a waste of time for your reader, but it might get confusing if all responses are not included or are not in the proper order.

BAD E-MAIL	GOOD E-MAIL
Re: Re: Re: Quarterly Meeting	Re: Re: Re: Quarterly Meeting
I vote for sales and product development.	You asked which teams should present to the board at the Quarterly Meeting – I vote for sales and product development.

3. Don't copy lots of people, but if you must, indicate why each person should care.

Does everyone really need to read this e-mail? We can cut down on overload one e-mail at a time. So think about who should get this e-mail and then let each recipient know why they have been included.

BAD E-MAIL	GOOD E-MAIL
TO: John, Jay, Joe, Jane	To: John, Jay, Joe, Jane

| Presentation is attached. | The presentation is attached. John – Do you feel comfortable with the slides? Be prepared to present the Introduction. |
| Let me know if you have any questions. | Jay – Be sure to bring the projector to the meeting. Joe – You might get product questions so be sure to review those slides for accuracy. Jane – FYI – If we close this deal, your team will have to work this weekend on the final proposal. |

4. Never bcc (blind carbon copy).

I'm sure you've heard the nightmares! If you want to let some-one else know about an e-mail conversation, do it in a separate forwarded e-mail. More often than not, the person who has been bcc'd does not realize it and they simply REPLY ALL, often to the shock of the recipient and embarrassment of the original sender. In other situations, the person who received the bcc has no idea why they have been included.

BAD E-MAIL	GOOD E-MAIL
TO: Christine FR: Randy BCC: Nichol	TO: Christine FR: Randy RE: Meeting to discuss 4Q Goals
Let's meet at 3:00 to discuss your challenges with 4Q goals.	Let's meet at 3:00 to discuss your challenges with 4Q Goals
	TO: Nichol FWD: Meeting to discuss 4Q Goals
	Please reserve the conference room for Christine and me for 3:00 – 4:00 today.

5. Clarify your requests.

If you're asking for action, make it clear to the reader. There's nothing more annoying to a reader than getting copied on an e-mail and finding out two weeks later that they were expected to fulfill some request hidden in the message. As the sender, you have only yourself to blame if you don't make your request clear. Summarize action items at the end of the message so that all recipients can easily read them at a glance.

BAD E-MAIL	GOOD E-MAIL
RE: New Phone system installation Nov 1	RE: New Phone system installation Nov 1
The telecom company will be here on Friday. Be prepared for the weekend installation.	The telecom company will be here on Friday. Jeremy – Prepare the final list of extensions. Carly – Notify all employees of the cutover schedule. Tom – Be available to meet with the technicians in case the systems are affected.

6. Edit forwarded messages.

Please review messages before you simply forward them on. Save the recipient from having to read through too much unrelated information. But even more important, save original senders from embarrassing or inappropriate comments not meant to be shared.

BAD E-MAIL	GOOD E-MAIL
TO: Jonathan	To: Jonathan

Let's go with Joe's idea to meet at Spago Restaurant (see below)	Let's go with Joe's idea to meet at Spago Restaurant (see below).
FR: Victor Let's have the meeting at the new Spago Restaurant. It has a great meeting space and *it's so expensive. This way we can get the company to pay for a great meal* :)	FR: Victor Let's have the meeting at the new Spago Restaurant. It has a great meeting space.

7. Be brief

Get to the point. No one wants to read a novel . . . they just want the facts. Remember, they're trying to get through their hundred e-mails, too. Make sure most (if not all) of your e-mail is visible in the preview pane. Most people never read past the first screen and very few will make it to the third.

And here's a writing tip: keep your sentences short, and do not have any paragraph longer than three lines. No one wants to get bogged down in an email. Make it easy for your reader to scan — and use bullet points whenever you can.

8. Communicate with people their way.

Some people love e-mail and respond all day long. Others, the more disciplined ones, check their e-mail periodically and respond as needed. And yet others don't enjoy e-mail at all and do most of their communicating via phone or instant messaging (IM). Before you get too frustrated because your e-mail has not been responded to within what you consider a reasonable period of time, find out how this other person operates. Try another method of communication. Pick up the phone or send an IM. Then ask them: "What is the best way to communicate with you? What if I need an urgent reply?" Remember that not everyone has the same habits as you.

9. Control yourself. Check e-mail only periodically during the day.

Why allow e-mail to interrupt you all day long? Remember Henry — the marketing specialist that went on to be the head honcho for his own company? He checked his email only several times a day. He was not its slave, but its master.

When you're meeting with someone, when you're working on a project, when you're focused on other important tasks, don't e-mail. Unlike face-to-face conversations and phone calls, people can communicate via e-mail independently. You pick the moments when to pay attention to e-mail. That's the beauty of e-mail.

But unfortunately, most people don't treat e-mail that way. They leave their e-mail "on" all the time, waiting with anticipation for each new arrival, each signaling to get your attention in case you're looking the other way. And many people can't help but allow themselves to be interrupted even for some meaningless message.

You have the power to control your e-mail interruptions. Either turn off the automatic checking feature completely or set it to something reasonable like every thirty minutes. Check your e-mail when it's convenient for you. Most e-mail doesn't require an immediate response. If the sender has something urgent to say to you, you will be found. We don't lack in methods of communication.

10. Ignore it.

Sometimes it's okay to simply ignore it, especially if the subject has no relevance to you. Don't just reply to get in on the conversation. And don't get involved if the matter can be handled by somebody else. Ignore and delete. If it's something really important, they will get back to you, you can be sure of that. And if someone did send you something that you feel compelled to ignore, then hopefully the senders will get the message and stop including you on irrelevant e-mails. This can only be good news for your personal IN box.

11. Never criticize someone in e-mail.

Somehow, negative feedback seems to get amplified by e-mail. Perhaps it's because the reader has the opportunity to read and re-read comments, allowing small nuances to grow with each reading. Needless to say, the bigger the audience the louder the criticism appears. It's guaranteed — nothing will get resolved through e-mail criticism. If this accidentally happens, a one-on-one conversation is immediately required; either in person or on the phone. Do not proceed via e-mail.

12. Informal is okay. Poor spelling and grammar are not.

Use correct grammar, spell check, and capitalize when appropriate. Remember, you are corresponding in a professional environment. Complete sentences make it easier to read and understand. When writing an e-mail that has a wide distribution and may be forwarded outside the company, be sure to re-read carefully before sending. It represents you.

13. No reply necessary.

Do you really need a response to every e-mail? Save your own IN box and save the recipient some time by flagging "No Reply Necessary," to those e-mails that don't require any action. This capability is simply activated in Microsoft Outlook in the drop-down section of the Follow-up flag by clicking on "Flag to Recipients." One less e-mail today, ten less tomorrow, and maybe one-hundred less e-mails for the week! Think of the possibilities! People only sending e-mail that is important — you get rid of clutter, fluff, aggravation; you get more production out of your day so you see more results.

14. E-mail is a public and permanent record.

E-mail may be stored on servers for years to come, whether you delete it off your system or not. This was a difficult lesson learned by executives at WorldCom, Enron and others. If you have something to say that you don't want known, it's better not said via e-mail.

These commandments come with a guarantee to improve your e-mail productivity. Only thing is, everyone has got to get on board. E-mail is communication. It takes two to tango and it takes two to have a conversation. You can do all the changing you want, but just like most changes, you can do them yourself and have some success, or you can get your whole team on the same page, and change the face of e-mail interaction. Start the revolution. Make these changes and watch as others catch on.

HOW MUCH IS THAT E-MAIL IN THE WINDOW?

Wonder how much your e-mail time is costing? Do a quick calculation:

1. Divide your yearly salary by 120,000 to get your per-minute wage.
2. Determine the average number of e-mails you process each day.
3. Multiply the number of e-mails by two. (Remember, studies show that each e-mail takes an average of two minutes.) This is your total daily minutes on e-mail.
4. Multiply the total daily minutes by your per-minute wage to find out what your e-mail time is costing you per day.
5. Multiply this daily cost by five to get your weekly cost.
6. Multiply by fifty (weeks) to arrive at your annual cost.

E-mail Cost Calculation

Salary: $100,000

Per minute wage: $100,000 / 120,000 = $.8333 per minute

100 E-mails per day x 2 minutes = 200 minutes/day

200 minutes x $.8333 = $166.66/day

Weekly cost = $166.66 x 5 days = $833.30 per week

Annual cost = $833.30 x 50 weeks = $41,665 per year

Back in chapter 5, the chapter on making a plan, I talked about how you can make decisions about whether something was important or not by how it affected revenue. If your e-mail usage is costing your company almost half your salary per year, then you better have something to show for it. Use your skills at making better decisions about how you spend your time and apply them to e-mail — all the time. Your company will appreciate it, and you'll have taken hold of the e-mail monster.

Start a Revolution

Be a leader. More than any other tip in this book, these changes need to happen company-wide to get maximum results. Get the e-mail revolution started today! Start sending better e-mails. Encourage your team to follow these commandments and slowly get the entire company on board. Better e-mail will result in better work every day.

Peak Performance Principles

▶ Think before you send. Will this e-mail do the job?

▶ Summarize in the Subject line.

▶ Control yourself. Check e-mail when it's convenient for you!

GERALD REALIZED, WITH GREAT DISMAY,
THAT HE HAD SPENT 8 HOURS READING
HIS SPAM BOX - NOT HIS INBOX.

CHAPTER 12
TO MEET OR NOT TO MEET,
THAT IS THE QUESTION

LET'S WORK TOGETHER
CANNED HEAT, 1970

Together we'll stand
Divided we'll fall
Come on now people
Let's get on the ball
And work together
Come on, come on
Let's work together

People who enjoy meetings should not be in charge of anything.
—Thomas Sowell

MEETINGS GET A BAD RAP FOR GOOD REASON

I've had countless people tell me that they'll go to a meeting and come out of it only to find that there needs to be another meeting to discuss what was decided at the first meeting. Meetings dominate the way we do business today. In fact, approximately 11 million meetings occur in the U.S. each and every day. Although many of us complain about meetings, we can expect to spend our careers deeply immersed in them.

But are we using our meeting time wisely? According to a white paper published by MCI (now Verizon, 1998): *Meetings in America: A study of trends, costs and attitudes toward business travel, teleconferencing and their impact on productivity*, most professionals attend a total of 61.8 meetings per month. That's two to three meetings a day! And what's worse, research indicates that over 50 percent of this meeting time is wasted. If e-mail is sucking half your time, then meetings account for a good third of what's remaining. It's no wonder we can't get any work done! Assuming each of these meetings is one hour long; professionals lose 31 hours per month in unproductive meetings. That's nearly four full working days.

Considering these statistics, it's no surprise that meetings have such a bad reputation.

So what are we doing about it? According to the same study, this is how professionals are reacting to this phenomenon every day:

► Daydreaming (91 percent)
► Missing meetings (96 percent)
► Missing parts of meetings (95 percent)

► Bringing other work to meetings (73 percent)
► Dozing during meetings (39 percent)

As a result, the majority of business meetings end up going in the wrong direction –

► Meetings are longer, less efficient and generate fewer results.
► More meetings are needed to accomplish stated objectives.
► With so much time spent in inefficient meetings, employees have less time to get their own work done.
► Ineffective meetings create frustration at all staff levels.
► Information generated at unproductive meetings usually isn't managed or leveraged properly.
► Inefficient meetings cost organizations billions of dollars each year in otherwise productive employee work time.

This situation is pretty serious. Meetings are meant to be important. They are there to keep you informed, exchange ideas, brainstorm and get your input on solving problems. They should be all about rocks and pebbles, but they have the tendency to turn into water. I would venture a guess and say that many professionals have never experienced the power of a truly effective meeting. Young professionals don't recognize the potential value of a well-organized meeting or perhaps even have the knowhow on how to run an effective meeting.

The good news is that good meetings are infectious. Once you start to run a good meeting generating real results, taking less time and accomplishing more, others will take notice, appreciate it, and likely mirror this behavior in their own meetings. The result is fewer meetings because those you do have are more productive, which adds up to extra time getting the important stuff done.

I'm certainly not recommending not going to meetings just because you don't find them meaningful. Instead, fight back by implementing the following Seven Rules of Productive Meetings in your organization and see a meeting's bad reputation turned to gold.

THE SEVEN RULES FOR PRODUCTIVE MEETINGS

1. Don't Meet

Avoid meeting if the same information can be covered in a memo, e-mail, or brief report. One of the keys to having more effective meetings is differentiating between the need for one-way information dissemination and a two-way information sharing.

If you want to be certain you have delivered the right message, you can schedule a meeting to simply answer questions about the information you sent. No need to rehash a report or read aloud as everyone sits around the table.

Don't meet because it's a habit or just the way you do things. Over time, daily, weekly or monthly meetings can become a habit instead of a planned activity with an expected outcome. Evaluate. Really find the honest answers to these questions: are your weekly staff meetings productive? Can you hold them less frequently and get the same or better results? Find the right balance between good communication and productive use of time.

2. Set Objectives for the Meeting

Before the meeting begins, even before planning the agenda, set your objectives for the meeting. Write down a phrase or several phrases to complete the sentence: "By the end of the meeting, I want the group to....." You can finish your sentence with comments such as: "Agree to at least five new features to add to the next version of our product;" or "Generate at least three new ideas for increasing sales into the healthcare sector;" or "Resolve the outstanding customer service issues we're having in the Northeast District."

One of the greatest benefits of setting objectives for a meeting is it helps you plan for a highly productive meeting. Your meeting objectives will form the basis of your agenda and will also help clarify who needs to be there.

Starting with an objective also has another powerful benefit. When you start a meeting with a clear objective, you can then evaluate your success at the end. With a stated objective, it's much easier to know if you actually met your objective or not. Then you can answer questions such as, "if not, why not?" Did your meeting get off track? Were the participants unprepared? This is worthy of discussion since it's in everyone's best interest to accomplish real results in every meeting where you spend both your and their valuable work time.

3. Provide an Agenda Beforehand

Provide all participants with an agenda before the meeting starts. As with your objective, the more specific you are with the agenda, the better your results. Be sure to include the following in the Meeting Agenda:

► Clear description of meeting objectives
► List of all topics and who will address each topic
► Timetable for each discussion point

Send out the agenda in advance, highlighting who is expected to present on which topics and indicating how the participants should be prepared to contribute to the meeting. No one should arrive at a meeting not knowing why they are there. If this is the case, they should take the initiative and find out so they can either be prepared or choose not to attend.

One good way to create an agenda that helps initiate discussion is to frame topics in the form of a question. For example, rather than the topic: "New product features" the agenda topic may be written as: "What new product features will help us penetrate the financial industry?" Questions often encourage readers to immediately think of answers.

If there is nothing on the agenda, the organizer should ask themselves whether there really needs to be a meeting at all.

Oh, and in pickle jar parlance, both the agenda and the objective can help meeting participants decide if the meeting is a rock, a pebble, important water or a complete waste of time. By keeping your focus in a meeting, the participants can keep focus in their day as well.

4. Assign Meeting Preparation

Giving all participants something to prepare for at your meeting will allow your meeting to take on a new significance to each team member. For problem-solving meetings, have the group read the background information necessary to immediately get down to business. Ask each group member to think of one possible solution to get everyone thinking about the meeting objective.

Consider starting all meetings on a positive note by having all participants recall their biggest success since the last meeting and ask one person to share their success with the group. Or ask each to think of one important thing accomplished since the last meeting. This will create the habit of demonstrated productivity within the group.

For less formal meetings or brainstorming sessions, ask a trivia question related to the meeting topic and give the correct answer in the first few minutes of the meeting. This is a sure-fire way to warm up the group and direct participants' attention to the meeting objectives.

▶

Meeting? Get Everyone Talking

▶ Start the meeting with a trivia question related to the content of the meeting: What is the purpose of this meeting? Ask everyone ... to ensure you're all on the same page.

▶ Good News! Have each participant share a recent success story. Set a positive tone.

▶ Brainstorm: Have everyone write down one solution or suggestion to the challenge at hand. Read the answers randomly and discuss the concepts.

▶ When disagreeing, respond back by paraphrasing the opposing view before presenting your own. It lets people know you understand them.

5. Stick to the Schedule

Start the meeting on time and end it on time, or better yet, end it early! Starting on time requires discipline by the organizer and the participants. Arriving late shows a lack of consideration for all those who were on time. But if all participants know that the organizer is going to start the meeting right on time, there is a much greater likelihood that everyone else will make the effort to be punctual.

Finishing in a timely manner is also critical. If everyone agreed that the meeting would last an hour, the meeting should not run any longer than that. Keeping the agenda realistic is as important to help make this happen as it is to staying on topic. Most groups have at least one person who tends to go off on a tangent or tell stories during meetings. Whether this is the organizer or one of the participants, all meeting participants have the responsibility to gently guide the meeting back to the agenda items and meeting objectives. But don't overreact. A little fun and levity always helps the process.

6. Assign Action Items

Don't move off any discussion in a meeting without deciding how to act on it. A discussion alone rarely resolves an issue. Decide immediately what the next step should be, who will be responsible for follow up, and by when. One meeting participant should carefully document the meeting and the assigned follow up.

Wrap up the meetings with a clear statement of the next steps. If any decisions were made at the meeting, even if the decision was "to study the issue more," the meeting organizer, or the person assigned to take meeting notes, should clearly summarize what decisions have been made, what the next steps are and who is assigned the responsibilities. This is crucial. If the participants leave the meeting and no one is accountable for taking action on the decisions that were made, then odds are the meeting will not have been worth everyone's time.

7. Examine Your Meeting Process

Assign the last few minutes of every meeting to review with the following questions: Did we accomplish the meeting objectives? What worked well in this meeting? How can we improve our next meeting?

Meetings are a fact of our work life. It is up to us to ensure they help us fill our personal jars with all the right stuff.

Peak Performance Principles

- ► Every meeting must have an Objective and an Agenda. Be sure everyone is aware of both.
- ► Stick to your schedule. Start on time. End on time.
- ► Get everyone involved: assign meeting preparation or start the meeting with something interesting or fun!

CHAPTER 13
THE PRESENT

IF I COULD SAVE TIME IN A BOTTLE

JIM CROCE, 1974

If I could save time in a bottle
The first thing that I'd like to do
Is to save every day
Till Eternity passes away
Just to spend them with you

If you want to make good use of your time, you've got to know what's most important and then give it all you've got.

—Lee Iacocca

I recently attended a professional seminar given by a professor of organizational development. He told us a wonderful story that made me pause for reflection. Not sure who the author is, but the message was crystal clear.

THE GIFT OF TIME

"Imagine there was a bank which credited your personal account each morning with a large sum of money. But, it carried over no balance from day to day. Every evening it deleted whatever portion of the balance you failed to use that day."

"What would you do?" he asked the audience. Everyone agreed they would draw it out, or use it all every single day.

"Well," he continued, "Each of you has such a bank, only instead of money, it credits you with time, exactly 1,440 minutes each and every day. Every night it writes off whatever you have failed to invest. There is no overdraft protection or carry-over of minutes.

"Each day you get a fresh deposit and each night you lose what you have not used. If you squander your deposit, you lose. If you invest well, you win.

"Invest your precious deposit in health, happiness and success. The clock is running. Make the most of today. And remember that time waits for no one.

"Yesterday is history. Tomorrow is a mystery. But today is a gift. That's why it's called The Present!"

Part Three

**A CULTURE
OF PEAK PERFORMANCE**

CHAPTER 14
RAISING EVERYONE'S GAME

WE ARE THE CHAMPIONS
QUEEN, 1977

We are the champions - my friends
And we'll keep on fighting - till the end.
We are the champions.
We are the champions
No time for losers
'Cause we are the champions - of the world.

A nation's culture resides in the heart and soul of its people.
—Mohandas Gandhi

THE ROAD TO PEAK PERFORMANCE

The business professionals who reviewed this book before it went to print, were from all types and sizes of organizations. One was from a regional bank, another from a medium-size software company, several from large corporations and a handful of professionals from a variety of small businesses. They all appreciated the material from their unique perspective and often focused on different concepts they felt would make the greatest impact on their own careers and their business environment.

But the two requests common to all were: (1) give the reader guidelines to develop their own peak performance habits and (2) give us some ideas on how we can share this information with others on our team so that our entire organization can benefit from these concepts. The more people are behaving with peak performance principles, the more success we can all have.

That's what this final section is all about. Take these ideas and make them an integral part of your personal behavior and your team culture. Modify them or change them completely to suit your style and the culture of your organization. But always keep your eye on the goal - to have everyone working at their peak performance level, which in the end, will help drive each individual's own peak performance.

Part Three really is its own entity. It's a workbook, and it is also available for download at www.PerformLikeA RockStarBook.com.

CREATE A NEW KIND OF CULTURE

Once your team begins to incorporate Peak Performance Principles into their daily routines and habits, productivity will improve, job satisfaction will increase, personal pride will develop and improved results will become evident pretty quickly.

The beauty of success is that it is infectious. Executives and other team managers will start to sense your team's new business style. People will notice the effectiveness of the meetings they run, the quality of the e-mails they send, the tight deadlines that are always met, and most importantly, your team's laser focus on the real priorities that get real results.

Start Slowly

The opportunity to develop and implement a corporate-wide Peak Performance initiative will gain traction once quality results have been demonstrated by your team. Consider introducing just a few Peak Performance principles to your team at a time. It is often best to implement just one or two of the concepts you think will have the greatest, impact first in order to demonstrate results and allow each person to experience their own sense of personal satisfaction and accomplishment. A slow introduction to a new culture of Peak Performance will ensure greater success since people's natural tendency is to resist changing their current behaviors and work habits.

A Culture of Peak Performance Will Emerge

Regardless of company size, all change must start at the top. New procedures implemented by the management team will be more quickly accepted by the entire corporate community.

Large and medium size companies typically implement by division, group, or department. For an effective Peak Performance Culture to emerge, new practices should be implemented across specific teams. When all team members simultaneously apply Peak Performance principles, each team's members stand to achieve the greatest results. When co-workers send better crafted e-mails, run much more results-oriented meetings, delegate effectively, and focus on the company's highest priorities, a corporate culture of Peak Performance will begin to emerge.

Small companies effectively develop a Culture of Peak Performance when training is implemented across the company simultaneously. It is not uncommon for employees in small companies to wear many hats and thus their daily interactions run across departments and functions. As a result, each employee typically impacts the workflow in several groups every single day. As with larger companies, when all team members apply these principles, everybody benefits and greater results can be achieved.

Make Changes Worthy of Big Results

Every company is different based on industry, size, geographic location, workflow, and certainly the personalities of its employees. So deciding which concepts to implement first is your unique and personal choice. If the Peak Performance Principles were first adapted by one group or department, evaluate their success to determine which specific techniques and concepts were immediately useful or had the greatest impact on personal productivity and organizational success.

To maximize employee acceptance and enthusiasm for developing a new Culture of Peak Performance, choose concepts that will be easy to learn and implement and will result in immediate success. Ease of implementation builds confidence and good results will develop a quick following for the new principles and business practices.

Be prepared to provide expected benefits of success. Demonstrate or discuss how the concept will specifically improve the current business environment or how it has already proven to be effective to teams that have already begun to implement the new business model. For example, if the team has implemented a model to replace one-hour meetings with forty-five or fifty-minute meetings and has discovered that not only are they getting more done in a shorter period of time, but on average, each person has "added" at least 1.5 working hours to their day – that's a story worth sharing.

Never Make Excuses!

Never allow an exception once you have decided to implement a Peak Performance practice. If you decide to implement the success principles of effective meetings, never accept a meeting request that does not include the objective of the meeting. The management team must discipline themselves and their teams to consistently implement the new practices. Do this every single day for at least three weeks until it becomes a natural way of doing business. It takes twenty-one days to develop a new habit pattern, and this is a good way to ensure that everyone develops good performance habits together.

Make It Fun. Reward Success. Reap the Benefits.

Nothing brings the team together like success and celebration. Let the team know that you are planning a Peak Performance Culture Celebration in forty-five or sixty days. The celebration will be a well-earned reward for working as a team to improve results and create a true Culture of Peak Performance. Have a party. Let the employees go home early, pass out freshly-baked chocolate-chip cookies with ice-cream. You can even create awards! I'm sure they will be proudly displayed outside cubicle walls alongside the weekly goal sheet. But whatever you do, make sure to throw in a little sand! Everyone will laugh, even cheer, and you will then know that your collective pickle jar is full up with all the right stuff.

CHAPTER 15
A PROGRAM FOR PERFORMANCE

HELP

BEATLES, 1965

Help, I need somebody,
Help, not just anybody,
Help, you know I need someone, help.

When I was younger, so much younger than today,
I never needed anybody's help in any way.
But now these days are gone, I'm not so self assured,
Now I find I've changed my mind and opened up the doors.

*I know you've heard it a thousand times before. But it's true
- hard work pays off. If you want to be good, you have to
practice, practice, practice.*

—Ray Bradbury

PERSONAL DEVELOPMENT OR TEAM TRAINING

The Peak Performance Program is a workbook with eleven separate discussion and activity sessions. You can choose to dive right into those specific areas you feel will yield the greatest and quickest return, or work through the topics in the order presented. The program can be used for personal development or as a group training exercise.

Personal development can be implemented individually, with another person or even in a group setting; providing mutual encouragement, motivation and support. Assuming everyone has read the book, participants can share experiences and success stories that relate to each topic and stimulate discussion and new ideas for dealing with the challenges of your distinctive business environment.

On the other hand, some professionals prefer to dissect the concepts on their own, thinking through each worksheet and developing a personal plan of action customized to their unique situation and goals.

Peak Performance Roundtable

You may choose not to use the worksheets, but rather implement a Peak Performance Roundtable based on group discussion. Here are some ideas for starting conversations that will engage everyone and build a learning environment that focuses on the key concepts in **PERFORM LIKE A ROCK STAR *and Still Have Time for Lunch.***

► Discuss the concept of peak performance in a jar.
- What are the components of your jar?
- Is this a work jar only? Are work and personal life integrated so all contents must be considered?
- Name the elements and assign actual goals, tasks and activities to each.

► Identify each person's individual goals and how they can be integrated into achieving excellence at work?
- How will the personal goals be accomplished by achieving success at work?
- How will achieving success at work impact the personal side of life?
- What specific actions can each individual take to move their personal goal along and improve their effectiveness at work?

► Discuss and identify the rocks, pebbles, sand and water in your life.
- List specific goals, activities and tasks applied to each area.
- How many do you have of each? Is there a balance?
- Evaluate what can realistically fit into the jar.

► How would you fill up the jar?
- Which rocks would go in first?
- Which pebbles are needed to support the rocks and make them happen?
- What should go in next and then last?

► What fun stuff is worth making time for?
- Consider fun stuff at work.
- Consider fun stuff at home.
- Consider fun stuff that is only for one's self.

► What low priority things can be eliminated?
  - Which ones can be modified, or done on a schedule?
  - Which ones can be delegated?

► Create a sample schedule... one that focuses on the important things, but is also realistic with the typical demands of the day.
  - Begin with the rocks (but not too many).
  - Include pebbles to support the rocks.
  - Leave room for sand and water.

► Select and discuss the top one or two challenges that are roadblocks to working at peak performance every day. (You can select from this list or identify your own.)
  - Taking control and responsibility for your time
  - Planning your work and working your plan
  - Identifying priorities
  - Setting deadlines
  - Defeating Procrastination
  - Creating and working from a prioritized list
  - Delegating
  - Handling Interruptions
  - Managing e-mail
  - Getting results from meetings

  - Review the chapter in the book that works through those challenges. Discuss why this challenge exists and come up with ideas to defeat it.
  - Write down effective techniques to better manage the situation.
  - Focus on one challenge at a time.

- Focus daily on Peak Performance in a Jar Theory, prioritizing and following the Rule of One: doing one thing every day of every week bringing you closer to your most important goal.
- Meet weekly to discuss progress; review results and benefits of new techniques.
- Have each individual teach their favorite technique to someone else—a great way to both learn and reinforce the concept.

THE PEAK PERFORMANCE PROGRAM

Use these *Discussions* as a guide. Implement a consistent program that introduces one concept at a time over an eleven-week period. Apply these concepts to real-life examples from your work environment and you will likely see yourself or your team adapt to peak performance techniques with enthusiasm. Success breeds success . . . and enthusiasm.

If you are working with a team, each week, prepare a list of discussion questions and share them with everyone in advance. Expect all participants to come with some discussion ideas. Encourage everyone to refer to the section in the book in preparation for the discussion.

DISCUSSION 1: PEAK PERFORMANCE IN A PICKLE JAR
(Refer to Chapters 1 & 2)

The Peak Performance Jar is a metaphor for your workday. You cannot change the amount of time available – it is always the same; but you do have the power to control how you fill your pickle jar and how you spend your time.

Discussion Questions & Activities:
- Demonstrate the Peak Performance concepts using the Pickle Jar Worksheet.
- Based on your (the team's) current goals and objectives, what are the priorities (rocks) that you are working on right now?
- Number and order these priorities with #1 being most important.
- If these goals and objectives are reached, write down how you/your team, department or company will benefit?
- What supporting programs, tasks and activities (pebbles) need to get done in order to accomplish the priorities listed?
- Are there challenges or roadblocks to the programs, tasks and activities that need to get done? What are they? How can you manage through those situations?
- What is the fun stuff (sand) that is part of the business day, but should not take priority? Some sand can be planned, like a pizza party reward for completing a large project; but other sand is individual such as taking care of personal business, working with co-workers, etc.
- Are there must-do's (water) you need to keep track of? How do you manage to keep track of these things without having them take over your day? (Example: Schedule approvals of Purchase Orders, responding to e-mail, managing meetings, etc.)

Fill Your Pickle Jar Worksheet

This is no ordinary pickle jar. This jar represents your time. Everyone has the same jar; it's how you fill it that makes all the difference. Fill it right, and you will have everything you want. Fill it wrong, and you will end up wasting your pickle jar, your time, and your day.

Identify the contents of YOUR pickle jar. Fill in the blanks and use this picture to guide you through your daily priorities and decisions.

ROCKS: Major goals, priorities, results-oriented activities

PEBBLES: Important tasks and activities that support your goals and priorities

SAND: Stuff we like to do, but should not take priority

WATER: The clutter - not fun, has to get done but never ends

ROCKS: _____

_____

_____

PEBBLES: _____

_____

_____

SAND: _____

_____

_____

WATER: _____

_____

_____

DISCUSSION 2: TURN GOALS INTO REALITY
(Refer to Chapter 3)

There is a lot of truth in the saying: 'So much to do, so little time.' Many people can never seem to accomplish all that they want to do in life – often because they are too busy working on the easy tasks, the fun stuff or simply those things that are the everyday details of living. It's time to take control and accomplish what you want. Start to make it happen today.

Discussion Questions & Activities:
- Share some "famous" stories or personal stories of people accomplishing their goals (sports figures, politicians, entrepreneurs, non-profit organizations, personal stories, etc.).
- How did these people accomplish their goals? Can you identify any "threads of wisdom" between the stories?
- What prevents you from pursuing your goals?
- How much time per day would you be willing to devote towards reaching your goals?
- How can we work together as a team to support each other's dreams?

Use these worksheets to help you understand your goals. I also challenge you to identify a breakthrough goal that may change your life and create a plan to make it real. Follow the simple steps and don't give up. If you work towards your dream you can realize it.

Top Ten Goals

Identify your top ten goals. Think ahead about what you might want to accomplish in the next two, five or ten years. No matter how difficult or farfetched, put your ideas down on paper. Writing them down will help you take an objective look and decide what you choose to focus on and what you choose to set aside.

List your top ten goals using the STAR method. Include a measurement and a time frame for each:

1. Goal: _____
   Measurement: Timeframe:

2. Goal: _____
   Measurement: Timeframe:

3. Goal: _____
   Measurement: Timeframe:

4. Goal: _____
   Measurement: Timeframe:

5. Goal: _____
   Measurement: Timeframe:

6. Goal: _____
   Measurement: Timeframe:

7. Goal: _____
   Measurement: Timeframe:

8. Goal: _____
   Measurement: Timeframe:

9. Goal: _____
   Measurement: Timeframe:

10. Goal: _____
    Measurement: Timeframe:

Top Three of Your Top Ten

Select the three most important goals. Consider these factors:
- Do I have the passion to pursue this goal?
- What would I gain if I achieve this goal?
- What would I sacrifice to achieve this goal or opportunity?
- Is the timeframe reasonable?

Top Three:

(1) _____

(2) _____

(3) _____

Create a Breakthrough Goal

Evaluate the goals you set. Review them and think about their potential to change your life. Is there one goal on your list that if you accomplished it, would change everything? A goal that would increase your income, improve your lifestyle, develop new relationships, put you or your business into a different category of success? This goal, that would break you through to the next level, is your breakthrough goal.

Write down your breakthrough goal:

_____

_____

_____

_____

_____

Write down how your business, income, opportunities, relationships, life – would change as a result of achieving this goal:

_____

_____

_____

_____

_____

_____

_____

_____

_____

_____

_____

_____

_____

_____

_____

_____

_____

_____

_____

_____

_____

_____

_____

Turn Your Goal into Action

It's wonderful to have a goal and the passion to make it happen. But in the end, every goal-setting exercise must be reduced to specific, concrete action steps that you can take to achieve your objective.

Step 1 - Clearly State your Goal: Document exactly what you are planning to achieve by what date:

_____

_____

_____

Step 2 - Develop a Strategy: What strategies can you apply to achieve this goal? List up to three strategies.

_____

_____

_____

Step 3 - Take Action: List specific action steps for each plan under each strategy. This list should be very long. But don't worry. You can apply the rule of one and make great progress over time.

Strategy: _____

Actions: _____

_____

_____

Strategy: _____

Actions: _____

_____

_____

Strategy: _____

Actions: _____

_____

_____

Strategy: _____

Actions: _____

_____

_____

Strategy: _____

Actions: _____

_____

_____

Strategy: _____

Actions: _____

_____

_____

Apply the Rule of One

Take ONE ACTION EVERY DAY towards achieving your goal.If you apply the Rule of One, you will have taken five actions a week, twenty actions a month and over two hundred actions each year towards achieving your goal!

DISCUSSION 3: PLAN YOUR WORK AND WORK YOUR PLAN
(Review Chapters 5)

It seems that the day has a mind of its own. As soon as you walk through the door, things happen: phones ring, e-mails pile up, people chat, priorities change and the important stuff doesn't get done. Not anymore! As of today – you will plan your work and work your plan.

Discussion Questions & Activities:
- How can you be sure to work on *your* priorities every day?
- What is the key question to ask when someone, even your boss, makes a request when you are working on a key initiative or priority?
- When is your best time to work on an important task?
- What are examples of some tasks and activities you should "plan" to accomplish?
- Whose priorities override yours?

Priority Planning Worksheet
The most important thing about a plan is having one. Be sure you not only have a plan, but you stick to it, even in the face of distractions and interruptions.

Use this calendar to evaluate your current reality and then create the reality you want:

Fill in your "Typical Day" in the section provided so you can face your own reality. Then choose to change it.

Now fill in Your NEW Day schedule:
- Select one, two or three important things you want to accomplish.
- Schedule them on the calendar.
- Select your Prime Time (if possible) for your important tasks.
- Let everything else fill in the remaining time slots.

Work a lot smarter by focusing on your priorities and you will achieve a whole lot more!

Time	Typical Sample Schedule	Your Typical Daily Schedule	Your NEW Daily Schedule*
8:00	Coffee, chat with co-workers		
9:00	E-mail		
10:00	Meeting		
11:00	Start Important Project. . . E-mail, Phone Calls, chat		
12:00	Lunch		
1:00	E-mail, Respond to others' requests		
2:00	Meeting		
3:00	Phone Calls, E-mail		
4:00	Chat, Help others		
5:00	Continue Important Project		

Schedule a maximum of two hours for your priorities and make the rest of the day flexible for all those things you know will crop up.

177

DISCUSSION 4: CREATE A TO DO LIST THAT PROMOTES ACTION
(Review Chapter 6)

All too often your To Do List is a project list. The problem with that is that every time you look at it — you get overwhelmed. Unless you have a lot of time, it's tough to cross the important things off. And therefore, you end up doing those quick, easy, unimportant tasks; and you've taken in a lot of sand and water. In the end, you've been very busy accomplishing very little.

What can you do about it? You can modify your list. Make your TO DO List an ACTION list that moves you forward on those important big projects.

Discussion Questions & Activities:

- How do you decide what to do if you don't have a To Do list?
- What is the best way to maintain a list?
- Is it better for you to have a To Do list of all your activities or a Daily Priority List?
- How do you turn your To Do list into an Action List?
- How has your To Do list helped you? Do you track the time it takes to complete a project? Do you prioritize by number? Do you cluster related activities? Share and discuss the team's own Best Practices.

CREATE YOUR ACTION LIST

Good organization is the hallmark of effective people; and the To Do List is the trademark. Every productive professional works from a prioritized To Do List. The key is to turn the list into action.

Convert you To Do List into your Action List.

Look at this sample classic To Do List and compare it to the Action List:

Classic To Do List	Action List	Time to complete
Product Brochure	• Research competitive product features • Identify key features for My Product • Talk to sales team about best selling features • Write copy	• 1 hour • 30 min • 30 min • 1 hour
Zenith Proposal	• Review Zenith RFP • Meet with product team to discuss best solution • Meet with finance to discuss pricing options • Write proposal	• 20 min • 30 min • 15 min • 1 hour

The classic To Do List has only two items – but each is a major project that requires a large chunk of time to tackle. By taking those major projects and breaking them into "next step" actions, the Action List is longer, but much easier to tackle in bits and pieces every day.

Take your To Do List and convert it into an ACTION list below. Use Action words that tell you exactly what you need to do to move forward on each task on the list. Indicate the approximate time it will take to complete the action to help you schedule your time.

My Classic To Do List	My NEW Action List	Time to complete

My Classic To Do List	My NEW Action List	Time to complete

DISCUSSION 5: DEFEAT PROCRASTINATION
(Review Chapter 7)

Everyone procrastinates. What can we do to ensure we move forward on those really important tasks because no matter how much we put them off, they won't go away?

Discussion Questions & Activities:

- Admit it – you procrastinate! What are your favorite ways to procrastinate? How do you procrastinate and still justify your actions as "work?"
- What are the two main reasons people procrastinate? Give examples the whole team can relate to.
- What is the first step to defeating procrastination?
- What is the second step to defeating procrastination?
- What is the third step to defeating procrastination?
- Give examples of how you can make this method work for you in this work environment.

Worksheet: I think I'll work on this later

Use this worksheet as your conscience! Fill it out. Put it on your wall. Let it jar you out of procrastination mode when you need it.

1) My favorite ways to procrastinate are:

2) The two reasons I procrastinate are:
   (1)

   (2)

3) How can I defeat procrastination? This is the 3-step process that works for me:
   (1)

   (2)

   (3)

4) My favorite rewards:

DISCUSSION 6: SET DEADLINES TO ACHIEVE RESULTS
(Review Chapter 8)

Deadlines are the magic that makes things happen. Without them, little would get done; but too many deadlines can cause frustration, stress and burn-out.

Discussion Questions & Activities:
- What deadlines can you apply to your current priorities?
- What deadlines can be applied to the tasks and projects that support those priorities?
- Can you modify these deadlines so they cause you to stretch, but not break, in order to accomplish these tasks and more?
- How can you make a public commitment to these deadlines to ensure you attain them?
- Identify routine tasks that you can assign deadlines to in order to move them along at a more efficient pace?
- Can you use deadlines to make your meetings more productive? (ex: shorter meetings; time-frames for discussions, etc.)

Deadlines: Love 'em or hate 'em — you need 'em!

There are lots of things on our plate that don't have specific deadlines. This is dangerous, very dangerous. These tasks and projects have the tendency to go on and on and on. Use this worksheet to create specific deadlines to help you move projects, activities and tasks along.

Task List *(sample)*	Deadline
Competitive Analysis	
▪ Complete review of Product A	January 15
▪ Complete review of Product B	February 3
▪ Create first draft of Competitive Analysis Report	February 15

YOUR Task List	Deadline

When you create and stick to your own deadlines, your manager will be impressed with your efficiency. You will feel proud of your accomplishment; and best of all, you will achieve a whole lot more!

DISCUSSION 7: DON'T LET INTERRUPTIONS GET IN YOUR WAY
(Refer to Chapter 9)

No matter your work environment or industry, there always seem to be those who have a habit of interrupting your thoughts and productivity. They constantly ask trivial questions or want to share every detail of their personal life. You don't want to offend them, but you have to do something. Discuss some diplomatic ways to deal with these situations.

Discussion Questions & Activities:

- How often do you get interrupted by chatterers in the office? What do you do about it?
- What is a good way to stop someone from chatting – and to send them away – without offending them? Give examples.
- What method can you use to diplomatically say "No" to a request? Give examples.
- In your effort to build relationships within your work environment you must always be considerate of others. How do you show that consideration?
- How can these concepts be applied in meetings? Discuss situations where attendees might get off topic or be long-winded with their comments.
- Discuss situations when you might be asked to take on a responsibility and feel uncomfortable saying "No" in front of the entire group. What are some of your ideas for handling these situations?

Worksheet : Mind if I interrupt for a minute? Actually, yes!

Discuss ways to diplomatically deal with people who:
- Interrupt you at a bad time.
- Tell you a long-winded story, when you don't have time to listen.
- Ask you to do tasks you don't want to do.

Fill out this worksheet so that you are prepared with the responses you feel most comfortable giving. Keep this where you can easily see it and refer to it discreetly when necessary.

Situation	How I can respond
Interruption	
Interruption	
Long-winded story	
Long bad attitude story	
Request I want to decline	
Other	

DISCUSSION 8: DELEGATE FOR BETTER RESULTS
(Refer to Chapter 10)

You can't do everything! By delegating to others you empower colleagues to take responsibility and free yourself up to focus on your priorities. Delegate well and everyone reaps the benefits.

Discussion Questions & Activities:

- What are good reasons to delegate?
- What tasks or activities should you never delegate?
- What are some key concepts to keep in mind to delegate effectively? Give concrete examples.
- Why do some people resist delegating? What is the problem with that?
- Give examples of delegating for results, not the process. Discuss why this can be a more effective way to delegate.
- Share examples of successful delegation that helped an employee learn, grow, develop self confidence, or experience another excellent result.
- What can you or should you delegate to free you up to work on more important tasks or projects?

Worksheet: Delegate for results

See the examples listed and create your own list. Remember, clearly communicate the results you expect, and then show your support by allowing the individual to accomplish those results their own way.

Who I delegate to?	What I delegate	Results I expect
Joy	Travel arrangements	-Aisle seat -Non-smoking hotel room
Steve	Partner Newsletter	-Delivered first Tuesday of every month -Include all product updates -Include at least two customer stories -Include at least 3 links to related resources
Sandra	Product Sales	-Attain monthly sales quota

DISCUSSION 9: MAKE THE MOST OF E-MAIL
(Refer to Chapter 11)

E-mail became prevalent little more than 20 years ago, but you can't live without it today.... not in your business dealings or your personal life. E-mail was the "killer-app" that created the computer revolution, but has it gone too far? Has e-mail productivity turned into inefficiency? How do you take full advantage of all e-mail has to offer while keeping it under control?

Discussion Questions & Activities:

- How many e-mails do you get each day? How many of them are really useful or important?
- Calculate the number of hours per day, week, month and year you spend on e-mail assuming that each e-mail takes an average of two minutes to handle. (This is the average based on quick responses.)
- What is your e-mail culture? To respond immediately? To copy everyone? To forward a long string to multiple people for feedback even if they have not been involved? Discuss the culture that exists today.
- What suggestions can the team offer to manage e-mail more productively? Which current cultural habits are you willing to give up or change in order to increase productivity?
- Review e-mail etiquette and give examples of the good and bad e-mails you have seen in the past week or month? How can the team implement this etiquette to enforce change?
- What does the team think are the top three etiquette ideas that will have the greatest impact on productivity? Will everyone commit to implementing these ideas without fail for the next month? At that time you can all discuss their effect and re-evaluate.

I Can't Live without E-mail!

Let's face it, you probably won't change all your e-mail habits overnight, but are you willing to change a few habits now that will make an immediate impact?

Make your mark. Check off at least three E-mail Commandments you commit to adhering to and watch both your own as well as your entire team's productivity improve.

	E-mail Commandment	I commit to do this	Initial & Date
1	Summarize every e-mail in the subject line		
2	When forwarding – summarize key points		
3	Do not copy lots of people unless necessary		
4	Never bcc		
5	Clarify your requests		
6	Edit forwarded messages		
7	Be brief		
8	Question: Is e-mail the best way to communicate?		
9	Control yourself – check e-mail only periodically		
10	Ignore it. You don't have to respond to everything		
11	Never criticize someone in e-mail		
12	Check your spelling		
13	Use the "no reply necessary" flag		
14	Never e-mail private information		

DISCUSSION 10: GET REAL RESULTS IN MEETINGS
(Refer to Chapter 12)

Meetings have evolved to be a larger part of business life than ever before thanks to technology that enables video-conferences, tele-conferences, webinars, virtual teams and, of course, the standard face-to-face meetings that occur daily in your office. With so much time spent "meeting" we must start focusing on outcomes that lead to results.

Discussion Questions & Activities:
- What meetings occur on a regular basis that might be easily replaced by an e-mail or less frequent meeting? (Example: weekly meeting replaced with bi-weekly meeting)
- What is the typical meeting time in your organization? Is this amount of time appropriate? If pushed to discuss the topic and resolve challenges more quickly, can the team do it? As a team, can you decide to cut down standard meeting times and give "everyone back" some time? (Example: All meetings will now be forty-five minutes so attendees get an extra fifteen minutes back from each meeting.)
- What type of advance preparation can help maximize results of meetings? Give specific examples of information distributed in advance that can help discussions be more meaningful and bring quicker resolution to challenges.
- Review the Seven Rules of Productive Meetings. Discuss how each rule can be applied to the current work environment.
- Which one or two rules can have the greatest impact? Commit to implementing and enforcing these rules within the team.
- Evaluate the results in thirty to sixty days. What worked? What needs improvement?

Worksheet: Put the Meat in Meetings!

Old habits die hard. As with e-mail, your company's meeting culture and e-mail habits will not be modified easily. So once again, don't try to change everything at once. Quite frankly, probably two or three slight modifications would make the biggest impact anyway. (Back to that faithful 80/20 rule: 20 percent of the changes you make will result in 80 percent of your improvement.)

Which changes are you willing to commit to? Mark them and make them happen!

	Meeting Rules	Commit to this	Initial & Date
1	Don't Meet		
2	Set Objectives for Meeting		
3	Provide an Agenda Beforehand		
4	Assign Meeting Preparation		
5	Stick to the Schedule		
6	Assign Action Items		
7	Examine Your Meeting Process		

DISCUSSION 11: IF YOU COULD CHANGE ONE THING, WHAT WOULD IT BE?

Clarity about what you want to accomplish is key to achieving it. Identify areas you want to improve and you will naturally focus on them and apply the techniques.

Fill in the blanks. What can you do in each of these areas to work a little smarter and accomplish a whole lot more?

- Master your day _____

- Focus on priorities _____

- Create a breakthrough goal_____

- Turn goals into reality _____

- Work your own plan _____

- Defeat procrastination _____

- Create a list that leads to action _____

- Delegate effectively _____

- Deal with interruptions_____

- E-mail for increased productivity_____

- Run meetings that generate results_____

Now, pick the one thing that will make the greatest impact and focus on it for a week. Master one virtue, go to the next, and then share what you know with others.

SHARE
Perform Like a Rock Star
and Still Have Time for Lunch

Who else can benefit from these Peak Performance Principles? Make a list of co-workers who would enjoy raising their game, taking on a new challenge and becoming more successful. And then circulate this book when you are done. Add a few names, and then pass it on. (Cross yourself off the list before you do.)

_____

_____

_____

_____

_____

_____

_____

_____

_____

Please return this book to: _____

Order your own copy at
www.PerformLikeARockStarBook.com

GIVE THE GIFT THAT ROCKS!

PERFORM LIKE A ROCK STAR
and Still Have Time for Lunch

Order online at: www.PerformLikeARockStarBook.com

Visit: www.PerformLikeARockStarBook.com
Visit: www.OrnaSpeaks.com

Drew Hyman

ORNA W. DRAWAS

International speaker and instructor for workshops on achieving high priority goals, Orna Drawas has worked to inspire thousands of business professionals in helping them drive towards real and measurable results in everything they do.

Serving as business coach to dozens of organizations in virtually every industry, Orna offers very practical approaches to attaining personal peak performance and real breakthrough results. By working closely with so many different professional organizations and environments, she has amassed an impressive understanding of the core principles that can truly make a difference for career-minded people in today's fast-paced and competitive environment. The result — *PERFORM LIKE A ROCK STAR and Still Have Time for Lunch.*

Contact Orna Drawas directly at www.OrnaSpeaks.com.

Book Cover and Layout Design: theBookDesigners
Cartoons: CartoonStock.com & NixComix
Cartoon of Orna: Nichol Ashworth
Picture of Orna: Drew Hyman